CW00376155

contents

It's time to get smart with the way we plan meals, the way we shop, how we store and prepare food to minimise waste, and how to make the most of the food we buy. These recipes will give you some great ideas on how to cook cleverly without breaking the budget.

Pamela Clark
Food Director

soups

scotch broth

1kg lamb neck chops
2.25 litres (9 cups) water
¾ cup (150g) pearl barley
1 large brown onion (200g),
   diced into 1cm pieces
2 medium carrots (240g),
   diced into 1cm pieces
1 medium leek (350g), sliced thinly
2 cups (160g) finely shredded savoy cabbage
½ cup (60g) frozen peas
2 tablespoons coarsely chopped
   fresh flat-leaf parsley

1 Combine chops with the water and barley in large saucepan; bring to the boil. Reduce heat; simmer, covered, 1 hour, skimming fat from surface occasionally. Add onion, carrot and leek; simmer, covered, about 30 minutes or until vegetables are tender.
2 Remove chops from soup mixture; when cool enough to handle, remove and discard bones. Chop meat coarsely.
3 Return meat to soup with cabbage and peas; cook, uncovered, about 10 minutes or until cabbage is tender. Sprinkle parsley over broth just before serving.

preparation time *30 minutes*
cooking time *1 hour 40 minutes* serves *4*
nutritional count per serving *25.9g total fat (11.4g saturated fat); 2278kJ (545 cal); 32.6g carbohydrate; 45.6g protein; 10.3g fibre*

Savoy is a large-headed, crimpled-leafed, loose-centred cabbage. It is less potent than other cabbages, so can be added to soups, stews and casseroles without fear of it overpowering the dish.

tuscan bean soup

chinese chicken and corn soup

tuscan bean soup

Use any thick-sliced bread you like; it must be dense enough so it doesn't break up in the soup.

2 tablespoons olive oil
3 medium brown onions (450g), chopped coarsely
2 cloves garlic, crushed
200g thick bacon pieces, chopped coarsely
2 medium carrots (240g), chopped coarsely
2 stalks celery (300g), trimmed, chopped coarsely
2 x 400g cans crushed tomatoes
¼ medium savoy cabbage (375g),
    shredded coarsely
1 medium zucchini (120g), chopped coarsely
2 sprigs fresh thyme
2 cups (500ml) beef stock
2 litres (8 cups) water
400g can borlotti beans, rinsed, drained
6 thick slices ciabatta bread

1 Heat oil in large saucepan; cook onion, garlic and bacon, stirring, about 5 minutes or until onion softens.
2 Add carrot, celery, undrained tomatoes, cabbage, zucchini, thyme, stock and the water. Bring to the boil then reduce heat; simmer, uncovered, 2 hours.
3 Add beans; simmer, uncovered, 20 minutes.
4 Meanwhile, toast or grill bread. Stand a slice of bread in the base of six serving bowls, top with soup. Drizzle with extra olive oil, if desired.
preparation time *15 minutes*
cooking time *2 hours 30 minutes* serves *6*
nutritional count per serving *11.8g total fat
(2.7g saturated fat); 1133kJ (271 cal);
22.9g carbohydrate; 14.1g protein; 8.3g fibre*

chinese chicken and corn soup

You need to buy a large barbecued chicken, weighing about 900g, to get the amount of chopped chicken needed for this recipe.

1 teaspoon vegetable oil
1cm piece fresh ginger (5g), grated
2 long green chillies, sliced thinly
2 x 505g cans chicken and sweet corn soup
2½ cups (625ml) water
3 cups coarsely chopped barbecue chicken
1 egg white
green onion, sliced, to garnish

1 Heat oil in large saucepan; cook ginger and chilli, stirring, about 2 minutes. Add soup, the water and chicken to pan; bring to the boil then simmer.
2 Beat egg white in small jug with 1 tablespoon of cold water then slowly pour into the soup, stirring constantly. Serve soup sprinkled with sliced green onion.
preparation time *5 minutes*
cooking time *15 minutes* serves *4*
nutritional count per serving *16.1g total fat
(2.4g saturated fat); 1037kJ (248 cal);
8.2g carbohydrate; 29.8g protein; 2.6g fibre*

meatball soup

4 Remove celery and carrots from stock; reserve. Leave bones in stock; cool stock. Strain stock into large bowl; discard bones and solids. Return stock, carrot, celery and undrained tomatoes to pan; bring to the boil. Reduce heat; simmer 15 minutes.
5 Meanwhile, cook pasta in large saucepan of boiling water until tender, drain; rinse under cold water, drain Add pasta and meatballs to soup; cook 10 minutes.

preparation time *20 minutes*
cooking time *1 hour 30 minutes* serves *6*
nutritional count per serving *15.5g total fat (5.4g saturated fat); 1359kJ (325 cal); 18.7g carbohydrate; 26g protein; 3.3g fibre*

curried cauliflower soup

1 tablespoon olive oil
1 medium brown onion (150g), chopped finely
2 cloves garlic, crushed
½ cup (150g) mild curry paste
2 litres (8 cups) water
1 small cauliflower (1kg), trimmed, chopped coarsely
2 medium potatoes (400g), chopped coarsely
1 tablespoon tomato paste
1 cup (250ml) buttermilk
½ cup loosely packed fresh coriander leaves

1 Heat oil in large saucepan; cook onion and garlic, stirring, until onion softens. Add curry paste; cook, stirring, 5 minutes.
2 Add the water, cauliflower, potato and paste to pan; bring to the boil. Reduce heat; simmer, uncovered, about 15 minutes or until vegetables are tender. Cool 15 minutes.
3 Blend or process soup, in batches, until smooth. Return soup to same cleaned pan, add buttermilk; stir over low heat until heated through.
4 Serve bowls of soup sprinkled with coriander and, if desired, accompanied with warmed naan bread.

preparation time *20 minutes (plus cooling time)*
cooking time *25 minutes* serves *6*
nutritional count per serving *12.1g total fat (1.8g saturated fat); 936kJ (224 cal); 16.8g carbohydrate; 8.3g protein; 6.8g fibre*

meatball soup

750g beef bones
2 medium carrots (240g), chopped coarsely
2 stalks celery (300g), trimmed, chopped coarsely
500g minced beef
1 egg, beaten lightly
½ cup (35g) stale breadcrumbs
1 tablespoon olive oil
410g can crushed tomatoes
½ cup (90g) small pasta

1 Place bones, carrot and celery in large saucepan, cover with cold water; bring to the boil, then simmer, covered, 1 hour, skimming fat from surface occasionally.
2 Preheat oven to 180°C/160°C fan-forced.
3 Meanwhile, combine mince, egg and breadcrumbs in large bowl. Shape heaped teaspoons of the mixture into small balls. Grease oven tray with oil; place meatballs, in single layer, on tray. Bake uncovered, 30 minutes, turning occasionally. Remove from oven; drain on absorbent paper.

curried cauliflower soup

lentil soup

lentil soup

1 tablespoon olive oil
1 medium brown onion (150g), chopped finely
1 stalk celery (150g), trimmed, chopped finely
1 medium carrot (120g), chopped finely
250g bacon bones
250g brown lentils
410g can crushed tomatoes
1 litre (4 cups) beef stock
2 tablespoons finely chopped
  fresh flat-leaf parsley

1 Heat oil in large saucepan; cook onion, celery and carrot, stirring, until onion is soft.
2 Add bones, lentils, undrained tomatoes and stock to pan. Cover; bring to the boil. Reduce heat; simmer, covered, about 1½ hours or until lentils are tender. Remove from heat; remove any meat from bones and add to pan, discard bones. Stir parsley through soup.
preparation time *20 minutes*
cooking time *1 hour 45 minutes* serves *4*
nutritional count per serving *8.6g total fat*
(1.8g saturated fat); 1342kJ (321 cal);
32.2g carbohydrate; 22.8g protein; 11.6g fibre

chunky beef and vegetable soup

2 tablespoons olive oil
600g gravy beef, trimmed, cut into 2cm pieces
1 medium brown onion (150g), chopped coarsely
1 clove garlic, crushed
1.5 litres (6 cups) water
1 cup (250ml) beef stock
400g can diced tomatoes
2 stalks celery (300g), trimmed, cut into 1cm pieces
1 medium carrot (120g), cut into 1cm pieces
2 small potatoes (240g), cut into 1cm pieces
310g can corn kernels, rinsed, drained
½ cup (60g) frozen peas

1 Heat half of the oil in large saucepan; cook beef, in batches, until browned.
2 Heat remaining oil in same pan; cook onion and garlic, stirring, until onion softens. Return beef to pan with the water, stock and undrained tomatoes; bring to the boil. Reduce heat; simmer, covered, 1½ hours.
3 Add celery, carrot and potato to soup; simmer, uncovered, about 20 minutes or until vegetables are tender.
4 Add corn and peas to soup; stir over heat until peas are tender.
preparation time *20 minutes*
cooking time *2 hours 10 minutes* serves *4*
nutritional count per serving *17g total fat*
(4.3g saturated fat); 1768kJ (423 cal);
26.7g carbohydrate; 36.9g protein; 7.5g fibre

chunky beef and vegetable soup

spiced coriander, lentil and barley soup

cream of pumpkin soup

spiced coriander, lentil and barley soup

Soup mix is a packaged blend of various dried pulses and grains, among them lentils, split peas and barley. It is available from supermarkets.

1 tablespoon coriander seeds
1 tablespoon cumin seeds
1 tablespoon ghee
6 cloves garlic, crushed
2 fresh small red thai chillies, chopped finely
1¼ cups (250g) soup mix
1 litre (4 cups) chicken stock
3½ cups (875ml) water
1 cup coarsely chopped fresh coriander
⅓ cup (95g) greek-style yogurt
1 tablespoon mango chutney

1 Dry-fry seeds in large saucepan, stirring, until fragrant. Using pestle and mortar, crush seeds.
2 Melt ghee in same pan; cook crushed seeds, garlic and chilli, stirring, 5 minutes.
3 Add soup mix, stock and the water to pan; bring to the boil. Reduce heat; simmer, covered, stirring occasionally, 1 hour. Cool 15 minutes.
4 Blend or process half the soup, in batches, until smooth. Return puréed soup to pan with unprocessed soup; stir over medium heat until hot. Remove from heat; stir in coriander.
5 Serve soup topped with yogurt and chutney.
preparation time *10 minutes (plus cooling time)*
cooking time *1 hour 20 minutes* serves *4*
nutritional count per serving *7.9g total fat (4.6g saturated fat); 1350kJ (323 cal); 49.7g carbohydrate; 11.4g protein; 3g fibre*

cream of pumpkin soup

40g butter
1 large brown onion (200g), chopped coarsely
3 rindless bacon rashers (195g), chopped coarsely
1.5kg pumpkin, chopped coarsely
2 large potatoes (600g), chopped coarsely
1.25 litres (5 cups) chicken stock
½ cup (125ml) cream

1 Melt butter in large saucepan; cook onion and bacon, stirring, until onion softens. Stir in pumpkin and potato.
2 Add stock, bring to the boil; simmer, uncovered, about 20 minutes or until pumpkin is soft.
3 Blend or process soup, in batches, until smooth. Return soup to same cleaned pan, add cream; stir until heated through.
preparation time *10 minutes*
cooking time *35 minutes* serves *6*
nutritional count per serving *20.6g total fat (12.2g saturated fat); 1534kJ (367 cal); 28g carbohydrate; 15.8g protein; 4.2g fibre*

beefy black-eyed bean and spinach soup

beefy black-eyed bean and spinach soup

You need 1kg of untrimmed spinach to get the amount of trimmed spinach required for this recipe.

1 cup (200g) black-eyed beans
1 tablespoon olive oil
1 medium brown onion (150g), chopped finely
1 clove garlic, crushed
2.5 litres beef stock (10 cups)
¼ cup (60ml) dry red wine
2 tablespoons tomato paste
500g piece beef skirt steak
250g trimmed spinach, chopped coarsely

1 Place beans in medium bowl, cover with water; stand overnight, drain. Rinse under cold water; drain.
2 Heat oil in large saucepan; cook onion and garlic, stirring, until onion softens. Add stock, wine, paste and beef to pan; bring to the boil. Reduce heat; simmer, covered, 40 minutes. Uncover; simmer 30 minutes.
3 Remove beef from pan. Add beans to pan; bring to the boil. Reduce heat; simmer, uncovered, until beans are tender.

4 Meanwhile, when cool enough to handle, remove and discard fat and sinew from beef. Chop meat coarsely; return to pan with spinach. Simmer, uncovered, until soup is hot.
preparation time *10 minutes (plus standing time)*
cooking time *1 hour 50 minutes* serves *4*
nutritional count per serving *13.9g total fat (4.2g saturated fat); 2199kJ (526 cal); 28.3g carbohydrate; 62.6g protein; 12.4g fibre*

minestrone

1 cup (200g) dried borlotti beans
1 tablespoon olive oil
1 medium brown onion (150g), chopped coarsely
1 clove garlic, crushed
¼ cup (70g) tomato paste
1.5 litres (6 cups) water
2 cups (500ml) vegetable stock
700g bottled tomato pasta sauce
1 stalk celery (150g), trimmed, chopped finely
1 medium carrot (120g), chopped finely
1 medium zucchini (120g), chopped finely
80g green beans, trimmed, chopped finely
¾ cup (135g) macaroni pasta
⅓ cup coarsely chopped fresh basil

1 Place borlotti beans in medium bowl, cover with water; stand overnight, drain. Rinse under cold water; drain.
2 Heat oil in large saucepan; cook onion and garlic, stirring, until onion softens. Add paste; cook, stirring, 2 minutes. Add borlotti beans, the water, stock and pasta sauce; bring to the boil. Reduce heat; simmer, uncovered, about 1 hour or until beans are tender.
3 Add celery to soup; simmer, uncovered, 10 minutes. Add carrot, zucchini and green beans; simmer, uncovered, about 20 minutes or until carrot is tender. Add pasta; simmer until pasta is tender.
4 Serve bowls of soup sprinkled with basil.
preparation time *20 minutes (plus standing time)*
cooking time *1 hour 50 minutes* serves *6*
nutritional count per serving *5.5g total fat (1g saturated fat); 1095kJ (262 cal); 39.9g carbohydrate; 9.4g protein; 6.5g fibre*

minestrone

chicken and vegetable soup

This soup needs to be started the day before serving.

1.5kg whole chicken
1 small brown onion (80g), halved
2 litres (8 cups) water
5 black peppercorns
2 bay leaves
20g butter
2 stalks celery (300g), trimmed, sliced thinly
2 medium carrots (240g), cut into 1cm pieces
1 large potato (300g), cut into 1cm pieces
150g snow peas, trimmed, chopped coarsely
3 green onions, sliced thinly
310g can corn kernels, drained

1 Place chicken, brown onion, the water, peppercorns and bay leaves in large saucepan; bring to the boil. Reduce heat; simmer, covered, 2 hours.
2 Remove chicken from pan. Strain broth through colander into large heatproof bowl; discard solids. Allow broth to cool, cover; refrigerate overnight. When chicken is cool enough to handle, remove and discard skin and bones. Shred meat coarsely; cover, refrigerate overnight.
3 The next day, heat butter in large saucepan; cook celery, carrot and potato, stirring, until onion softens.
4 Discard fat from surface of broth, add broth to pan; bring to the boil. Reduce heat; simmer, covered, about 10 minutes or until vegetables are just tender.
5 Add snow peas, green onion, corn and reserved chicken meat to soup; cook, covered, 5 minutes or until heated through.

preparation time *20 minutes (plus refrigeration)*
cooking time *2 hours 40 minutes* serves *6*
nutritional count per serving *9.2g total fat
(2.8g saturated fat); 1183kJ (283 cal);
18.8g carbohydrate; 29.1g protein; 4.2g fibre*

vegetable soup

You need approximately 1kg untrimmed silver beet to get the amount of trimmed silver beet required for this recipe.

1 tablespoon vegetable oil
2 large brown onions (400g), chopped finely
2 large carrots (360g), chopped coarsely
8 stalks celery (1.2kg), trimmed,
  chopped coarsely
3 cloves garlic, crushed
1 litre (4 cups) vegetable stock
1 litre (4 cups) water
¾ cup (165g) risoni pasta
2 medium zucchini (240g), sliced thickly
250g trimmed silver beet, chopped coarsely

1 Heat oil in large saucepan; cook onion, carrot, celery and garlic, stirring, until vegetables soften.
2 Add stock and the water to pan; bring to the boil. Reduce heat; simmer, uncovered, 10 minutes. Add pasta and zucchini; simmer, uncovered, stirring occasionally, about 5 minutes or until pasta is tender. Add silver beet; cook, stirring, until silver beet just wilts.

preparation time *15 minutes*
cooking time *35 minutes* serves *4*
nutritional count per serving *6.8g total fat (1.2g saturated fat); 1296kJ (310 cal); 43.5g carbohydrate; 12.4g protein; 11.5g fibre*

cream of kumara soup with rosemary sourdough

pea and ham soup

cream of kumara soup with rosemary sourdough

1 tablespoon olive oil
2 medium kumara (800g), chopped coarsely
1 medium brown onion (150g), chopped coarsely
2 cloves garlic, quartered
2 teaspoons coarsely chopped fresh rosemary
1 teaspoon finely grated lemon rind
2 cups (500ml) vegetable stock
2 cups (500ml) water
1 tablespoon lemon juice
½ cup (125ml) cream

1 Heat oil in large frying pan; cook kumara, onion and garlic, stirring, 10 minutes. Add rosemary, rind, stock and the water; bring to the boil. Reduce heat; simmer, covered, about 15 minutes or until kumara is soft. Cool 15 minutes.
2 Meanwhile, make rosemary sourdough.
3 Blend or process soup, in batches, until smooth. Return soup to same cleaned pan, add juice; stir over medium heat until hot.
4 Serve bowls of soup drizzled with cream and accompanied with sourdough.
preparation time *10 minutes (plus cooling time)*
cooking time *30 minutes* serves *6*
nutritional count per serving *25.8g total fat (8.4g saturated fat); 2982kJ (713 cal); 96.2g carbohydrate; 18g protein; 11.4g fibre*

rosemary sourdough

2 tablespoons olive oil
2 teaspoons finely chopped fresh rosemary
1 loaf sourdough bread (675g),
  sliced into 3cm pieces

1 Preheat oven to 180°C/160°C fan-forced.
2 Combine oil and rosemary in large bowl; add bread, turn to coat in mixture. Place bread on oven tray; toast bread, both sides, about 15 minutes.

pea and ham soup

Risoni, a small rice-shaped pasta, is often used as the pasta of choice when making soup.

2 teaspoons olive oil
1 medium brown onion (150g), chopped coarsely
2 teaspoons ground cumin
2.5 litres (10 cups) water
2 stalks celery (300g), trimmed, chopped coarsely
2 dried bay leaves
1.5kg ham bone
1 cup (220g) risoni pasta
2 cups (240g) frozen peas
2 tablespoons finely chopped fresh mint

1 Heat oil in large saucepan; cook onion, stirring, until softened. Add cumin; cook, stirring, until fragrant. Add the water, celery, bay leaves and ham bone; bring to the boil. Reduce heat; simmer, covered, 1 hour, skimming fat from surface occasionally.
2 Remove bone; when cool enough to handle, remove meat from bone, discard skin and fat. Shred ham finely.
3 Return soup to the boil; stir in ham, pasta and peas. Cook, uncovered, about 5 minutes or until pasta is tender. Sprinkle soup with mint to serve.
preparation time *15 minutes*
cooking time *1 hour 15 minutes* serves *6*
nutritional count per serving *3g total fat (0.6g saturated fat); 811kJ (194 cal); 30g carbohydrate; 9g protein; 4.6g fibre*

lamb shank and vegetable soup

lamb shank and vegetable soup

4 lamb shanks (1kg)
2 medium carrots (240g), chopped coarsely
2 medium brown onions (300g), chopped coarsely
2 cloves garlic, crushed
2 medium potatoes (400g), chopped coarsely
2 stalks celery (300g), trimmed, chopped coarsely
400g can chopped tomatoes
1.5 litres (6 cups) beef or chicken stock
½ cup (140g) tomato paste
2 medium zucchini (240g), chopped coarsely

1 Place shanks, carrot, onion, garlic, potato, celery, undrained tomatoes, stock and paste in large saucepan; bring to the boil. Reduce heat; simmer, covered, 1 hour.
2 Add zucchini to soup, simmer, uncovered, further 30 minutes or until shanks are tender.
3 Remove shanks from soup. When cool enough to handle, remove meat from bones, discard bones. Return meat to soup; stir until heated through.
preparation time *20 minutes*
cooking time *1 hour 40 minutes* serves 4
nutritional count per serving *9.2g total fat (3.9g saturated fat); 1513kJ (362 cal); 29.2g carbohydrate; 39.7g protein; 8.5g fibre*

lamb and barley soup

You need approximately 1kg untrimmed silver beet to get the amount of trimmed silver beet required for this recipe.
You could also use 2kg lamb neck chops instead of the lamb shanks in this soup. Cut any excess fat from the meat before you cook it or skim any fat off the soup's surface as it is cooking.

1.5kg french-trimmed lamb shanks
3 litres (12 cups) water
¾ cup (150g) pearl barley
1 medium carrot (120g), sliced thinly
1 medium leek (350g), sliced thinly
2 stalks celery (300g), trimmed, sliced thinly
1 tablespoon curry powder
250g trimmed silver beet, chopped coarsely

1 Combine shanks, the water and barley in large saucepan; bring to the boil. Reduce heat; simmer, uncovered, 1 hour, skimming fat from surface occasionally. Add carrot, leek and celery; simmer, uncovered, 10 minutes.
2 Remove shanks from soup mixture. When cool enough to handle, remove meat; chop coarsely. Discard bones and any fat or skin.
3 Dry-fry curry powder in small saucepan until fragrant. Return meat to soup with curry powder and silver beet; cook, uncovered, until silver beet just wilts.
preparation time *15 minutes*
cooking time *1 hour 25 minutes* serves 6
nutritional count per serving *13.3g total fat (5.7g saturated fat); 1404kJ (336 cal); 18.9g carbohydrate; 31.8g protein; 6.4g fibre*

lamb and barley soup

french onion soup with gruyère croûtons

50g butter
4 large brown onions (800g), halved, sliced thinly
¾ cup (180ml) dry white wine
3 cups (750ml) water
1 litre (4 cups) beef stock
1 bay leaf
1 tablespoon plain flour
1 teaspoon fresh thyme leaves

1 Melt butter in large saucepan; cook onion, stirring, about 30 minutes or until caramelised.
2 Meanwhile, bring wine to the boil in large saucepan; boil 1 minute. Stir in the water, stock and bay leaf; return to the boil. Remove from heat.
3 Stir flour into onion mixture; cook, stirring, 2 minutes. Gradually add hot broth mixture, stirring, until mixture boils and thickens slightly. Reduce heat; simmer, uncovered, stirring occasionally, 20 minutes. Discard bay leaf; stir in thyme.
4 Meanwhile, make gruyère croûtons.
5 Serve bowls of soup topped with croûtons.
preparation time *30 minutes*
cooking time *50 minutes* serves *4*
nutritional count per serving *6.8g total fat (3.7g saturated fat); 719kJ (172 cal); 18g carbohydrate; 7.1g protein; 1.5g fibre*

gruyère croûtons

1 small french bread stick (150g)
½ cup (60g) finely grated gruyère cheese

1 Preheat grill.
2 Cut bread stick into 1.5cm slices; discard end pieces. Toast slices one side then turn and sprinkle equal amounts of cheese over untoasted sides; grill croûtons until cheese browns lightly.

potato and leek soup with croûtons

1 tablespoon olive oil
50g butter
4 medium potatoes (800g), chopped coarsely
1 large leek (500g), sliced thickly
300ml cream
2 tablespoons finely chopped fresh chives
1 tablespoon finely chopped fresh basil
1 tablespoon finely chopped fresh dill
vegetable broth
2 medium potatoes (400g), chopped coarsely
2 medium carrots (240g), chopped coarsely
1 large brown onion (200g), chopped coarsely
1 medium tomato (150g), chopped coarsely
1 stalk celery (150g), trimmed, chopped coarsely
1.5 litres (6 cups) water

1 Make vegetable broth.
2 Heat oil and butter in same cleaned pan; cook potato and leek, covered, 15 minutes, stirring occasionally. Add broth; bring to the boil. Reduce heat; simmer, covered, 15 minutes. Cool 15 minutes.
3 Meanwhile, make croûtons.
4 Blend or process soup, in batches, until smooth. Return soup to same cleaned pan, add cream; stir over medium heat until hot.
5 Serve bowls of soup sprinkled with combined herbs and topped with croûtons.
vegetable broth Combine ingredients in large saucepan; bring to the boil. Reduce heat; simmer, uncovered, 20 minutes. Strain broth through muslin-lined sieve or colander into large heatproof bowl; discard solids.

preparation time *30 minutes (plus cooling time)*
cooking time *55 minutes* serves *4*
nutritional count per serving *58.6g total fat (35.6g saturated fat); 3357kJ (802 cal); 52.5g carbohydrate; 2.6g protein; 10.8g fibre*

croûtons

2 slices wholemeal bread (90g)
50g butter

1 Cut and discard crusts from bread; cut bread into 1cm pieces.
2 Melt butter in medium frying pan. Add bread; cook, stirring, until croûtons are browned lightly. Drain on absorbent paper.

pasta & pizza

spaghetti bolognese

1 tablespoon olive oil
2 large brown onions (400g), chopped finely
4 cloves garlic, crushed
1.2kg beef mince
2 large carrots (360g), grated coarsely
⅓ cup (95g) tomato paste
3 cups (750ml) beef stock
2 x 810g cans crushed tomatoes
1 tablespoon mixed dried herbs
500g spaghetti

1 Heat oil in large saucepan; cook onion and garlic, stirring, until onion softens.
2 Add mince to pan; cook, stirring, until browned. Add carrot and paste; cook, stirring, 5 minutes. Add stock, undrained tomato and herbs; bring to the boil. Reduce heat; simmer, covered, 45 minutes, stirring occasionally. Uncover; simmer, about 45 minutes or until thickened slightly.
3 About 10 minutes before sauce is ready, cook pasta in large saucepan of boiling water until just tender; drain.
4 Serve half the bolognese with spaghetti; sprinkle with grated parmesan, if you like. Freeze remaining bolognese sauce.

preparation time *15 minutes*
cooking time *1 hour 40 minutes* serves *4*
nutritional count per serving *39.8g total fat (15.2g saturated fat); 4836kJ (1157 cal); 110g carbohydrate; 81.8g protein; 13.7g fibre*

This recipe makes a double quantity of bolognese sauce; use half for this recipe and store the remainder in the freezer for up to 3 months for later use.

rigatoni with eggplant sauce

3 Meanwhile, cook pasta in large saucepan of boiling water until tender; drain. Place pasta in large bowl with half the eggplant sauce; toss gently to combine. Divide pasta among serving plates; top each with remaining sauce and cheese.

preparation time *10 minutes*
cooking time *20 minutes* serves *4*
nutritional count per serving *17.9g total fat (3.3g saturated fat); 2625kJ (628 cal); 88.1g carbohydrate; 17.5g protein; 10.8g fibre*

bucatini with moroccan lamb sauce

You can use plain spaghetti instead of the bucatini.

2 teaspoons olive oil
1 small brown onion (80g), chopped finely
2 cloves garlic, crushed
500g minced lamb
1 teaspoon ground cumin
½ teaspoon ground cayenne pepper
½ teaspoon ground cinnamon
2 tablespoons tomato paste
2 x 415g cans crushed tomatoes
1 large zucchini (150g), chopped coarsely
2 tablespoons finely chopped fresh mint
375g bucatini pasta

1 Heat oil in large saucepan; cook onion and garlic, stirring, until onion softens. Add mince; cook, stirring, until changed in colour. Add spices; cook, stirring, until fragrant.
2 Stir in paste, undrained tomatoes and zucchini; bring to the boil. Reduce heat; simmer, uncovered, about 15 minutes or until sauce thickens slightly. Stir in mint.
3 Meanwhile, cook pasta in large saucepan of boiling water until tender; drain. Serve pasta topped with sauce.
preparation time *10 minutes*
cooking time *20 minutes* serves *4*
nutritional count per serving *16.2g total fat (6.3g saturated fat); 2562kJ (613 cal); 73.4g carbohydrate; 38.9g protein; 7.3g fibre*

rigatoni with eggplant sauce

¼ cup (60ml) olive oil
1 medium brown onion (150g), chopped finely
2 stalks celery (300g), trimmed, chopped finely
1 clove garlic, crushed
2 tablespoons brandy, optional
1 medium eggplant (300g), sliced thinly
600ml bottled tomato pasta sauce
½ cup (140g) tomato paste
½ cup (125ml) water
375g rigatoni pasta
¼ cup (20g) finely grated parmesan cheese

1 Heat oil in large saucepan; cook onion, celery and garlic, stirring, until onion softens. Add brandy; cook, stirring, until brandy evaporates. Add eggplant; cook, stirring, until eggplant is tender.
2 Stir in sauce, paste and the water; bring to the boil. Reduce heat; simmer, uncovered, about 10 minutes or until sauce thickens slightly.

bucatini with moroccan lamb sauce

macaroni cheese

This quick version doesn't have to go into the oven like traditional macaroni cheese, so it's great when you want dinner on the table fast.

250g elbow macaroni pasta
60g butter
⅓ cup (50g) plain flour
3 cups (750ml) milk
2 cups (220g) coarsely grated pizza cheese

1 Cook pasta in large saucepan of boiling water until tender; drain.

2 Meanwhile, melt butter in medium saucepan, add flour; cook, stirring, about 2 minutes or until mixture thickens and bubbles. Gradually stir in milk; cook, stirring, until sauce boils and thickens. Stir pasta and half the cheese into sauce.

3 Preheat grill.

4 Pour mixture into shallow 2-litre (8-cup) baking dish. Sprinkle with remaining cheese; place under hot grill until cheese melts and is browned lightly.

preparation time *5 minutes*
cooking time *20 minutes* serves *4*
nutritional count per serving *32.5g total fat (20.8g saturated fat); 2776kJ (664 cal); 60.8g carbohydrate; 30.7g protein; 2.5g fibre*

pea and salmon pasta bake

375g rigatoni pasta
40g butter
2 tablespoons plain flour
2 cups (500ml) milk
1½ cups (180g) frozen peas
½ cup (40g) coarsely grated parmesan cheese
1¼ cups (160g) coarsely grated
    cheddar cheese
415g can pink salmon, drained,
    skin and bones removed

1 Preheat oven to 200°C/180°C fan-forced.
2 Cook pasta in large saucepan of boiling water until tender; drain.
3 Meanwhile, melt butter in medium saucepan, add flour; cook, stirring, until mixture thickens and bubbles. Gradually add milk; cook, stirring, over medium heat, until sauce boils and thickens. Stir in peas, ¼ cup parmesan and ¾ cup cheddar.
4 Combine sauce mixture with pasta and salmon in shallow 2.5-litre (10-cup) oiled ovenproof dish; sprinkle with remaining combined cheeses. Bake, uncovered, in oven, about 20 minutes or until browned lightly.

preparation time *15 minutes*
cooking time *35 minutes* serves *6*
nutritional count per serving *24.4g total fat (14.1g saturated fat); 2370kJ (567 cal); 51.2g carbohydrate; 33.6g protein; 3.9g fibre*

fettuccine alfredo

spaghetti puttanesca

Sauce can be made two days ahead; store, covered, in the refrigerator.

375g spaghetti
¼ cup (60ml) olive oil
2 cloves garlic, crushed
4 medium tomatoes (600g), chopped coarsely
½ cup finely chopped fresh flat-leaf parsley
12 stuffed olives, sliced thinly
45g can anchovy fillets, chopped finely
1 tablespoon finely shredded fresh basil
pinch chilli powder

1 Cook pasta in large saucepan of boiling water until tender; drain.
2 Meanwhile, heat oil in medium frying pan; cook garlic until it just changes colour. Add tomato, parsley, olives, anchovy, basil and chilli powder; cook, stirring, 5 minutes. Combine sauce and pasta.
preparation time *15 minutes*
cooking time *15 minutes* serves *4*
nutritional count per serving *16.9g total fat (2.5g saturated fat); 2073kJ (496 cal); 67.2g carbohydrate; 15.2g protein; 6.5g fibre*

fettuccine alfredo

375g fettuccine pasta
90g butter
⅔ cup (160ml) cream
1 cup (80g) grated parmesan cheese
1 tablespoon finely chopped fresh flat-leaf parsley

1 Cook pasta in large saucepan of boiling water until tender; drain.
2 Meanwhile, heat butter and cream in medium frying pan until butter melts; remove from heat. Add cheese and parsley; stir until sauce is blended and smooth.
3 Combine sauce and pasta; sprinkle with chopped parsley, if desired.
preparation time *5 minutes*
cooking time *15 minutes* serves *4*
nutritional count per serving *43.2g total fat (27.9g saturated fat); 3056kJ (731 cal); 65.3g carbohydrate; 19g protein; 3.2g fibre*

spaghetti puttanesca

macaroni tuna salad

Yellow string beans are sometimes called butter beans; you can substitute them with chopped snake beans, a long (about 40cm) fresh green bean.

250g small macaroni pasta
200g green beans, halved
200g yellow string beans, halved
415g can tuna in oil, drained, flaked
1 small red onion (100g), sliced thinly
¼ cup loosely packed, finely chopped
    fresh flat-leaf parsley
½ cup (125ml) olive oil
¼ cup (60ml) lemon juice
2 cloves garlic, crushed
2 teaspoons curry powder

1 Cook pasta in large saucepan of boiling water until tender; drain. Rinse under cold water; drain.
2 Meanwhile, boil, steam or microwave beans until just tender; drain. Rinse under cold water; drain.
3 Place pasta and beans in large bowl with tuna, onion, parsley and combined remaining ingredients; toss gently to combine.

preparation time *15 minutes*
cooking time *15 minutes* serves *4*
nutritional count per serving *41g total fat (6g saturated fat); 2880kJ (689 cal); 47.2g carbohydrate; 30.4g protein; 5.8g fibre*

penne arrabiata

375g penne pasta
1 tablespoon olive oil
2 medium brown onions (300g), chopped finely
5 cloves garlic, crushed
3 fresh small red thai chillies, chopped finely
600ml bottled tomato pasta sauce
2 teaspoons balsamic vinegar
¼ cup (20g) finely grated parmesan cheese

1 Cook pasta in large saucepan of boiling water until tender; drain.
2 Meanwhile, heat oil in large saucepan; cook onion, garlic and chilli, stirring, until onion softens. Add sauce and vinegar; bring to the boil, then simmer, uncovered, about 5 minutes or until sauce thickens slightly. Combine pasta with sauce; sprinkle with cheese to serve.

preparation time *10 minutes*
cooking time *15 minutes* serves *4*
nutritional count per serving *8.6g total fat
(2.1g saturated fat); 2082kJ (498 cal);
84.2g carbohydrate; 16g protein; 7.8g fibre*

spaghetti siciliana

penne matriciana

spaghetti siciliana

45g can anchovy fillets, drained
2 tablespoons milk
⅓ cup (80ml) olive oil
1 medium brown onion (150g), grated
1 small eggplant (230g), chopped finely
1 small green capsicum (150g), chopped finely
2 cloves garlic, crushed
2 x 410g cans crushed tomatoes
1 teaspoon finely chopped fresh basil
10 seeded black olives, chopped finely
1 tablespoon capers, rinsed, drained,
    chopped finely
¼ cup finely chopped fresh flat-leaf parsley
375g spaghetti

1 Place anchovies in small shallow bowl. Cover with milk; stand 10 minutes to remove excessive salty taste. Drain well; chop anchovies finely.
2 Heat oil in large frying pan. Cook onion, eggplant and capsicum, stirring, until eggplant is soft; add garlic, undrained tomatoes and basil. Cover; bring to the boil. Reduce heat; simmer, covered, 30 minutes. Add anchovy, olives, capers and parsley; cook, uncovered, a further 5 minutes.
3 Meanwhile, cook pasta in large saucepan of boiling water until tender; drain. Serve sauce over pasta.

preparation time *20 minutes*
cooking time *45 minutes* serves 4
nutritional count per serving *21.2g total fat*
(3.2g saturated fat); 2454kJ (587 cal);
78.2g carbohydrate; 16.4g protein; 8.3g fibre

penne matriciana

375g penne pasta
1 tablespoon olive oil
1 medium brown onion (150g), chopped finely
6 rindless bacon rashers (520g), sliced thinly
2 large tomatoes (440g), peeled,
    chopped coarsely
1 fresh small red thai chilli, chopped finely

1 Cook pasta in large saucepan of boiling water until tender; drain.
2 Meanwhile, heat oil in large frying pan; cook onion and bacon over medium heat, stirring, about 5 minutes or until onion is soft. Drain excess fat. Stir in tomato and chilli. Simmer sauce, gently, uncovered, 5 minutes, stirring occasionally. Combine sauce with pasta.

preparation time *20 minutes*
cooking time *10 minutes* serves 4
nutritional count per serving *23.6g total fat*
(7.2g saturated fat); 2696kJ (645 cal);
68.9g carbohydrate; 37.4g protein; 5.1g fibre

bow ties and salmon in lemon cream

bow ties and salmon in lemon cream

Bow ties, also known as farfalle or butterfly pasta, is a bow-tie shaped short pasta.

375g bow tie pasta
1 medium lemon (140g)
415g can red salmon, drained, flaked
½ cup (125ml) cream
4 green onions, sliced thinly

1 Cook pasta in large saucepan of boiling water until tender; drain.
2 Meanwhile, using zester, remove rind from lemon. Place rind and pasta in large saucepan with remaining ingredients; stir over low heat until hot.
preparation time *10 minutes*
cooking time *15 minutes* serves *4*
nutritional count per serving *20.1g total fat (10.7g saturated fat); 2404kJ (575 cal); 65.9g carbohydrate; 29.9g protein; 4.2g fibre*

angel hair frittata

100g angel hair pasta
1 tablespoon vegetable oil
1 small leek (200g), chopped coarsely
2 cloves garlic, crushed
¼ cup (20g) finely grated parmesan cheese
200g fetta cheese, crumbled
60g spinach leaves, chopped coarsely
½ cup (120g) sour cream
¼ teaspoon ground nutmeg
6 eggs, beaten lightly

1 Cook pasta in large saucepan of boiling water, uncovered, until just tender; drain.
2 Meanwhile, heat oil in 20cm-base frying pan; cook leek and garlic, stirring, until leek softens.
3 Combine pasta and leek mixture in large bowl with cheeses, spinach, sour cream, nutmeg and egg. Pour mixture into same frying pan, cover; cook over low heat for 10 minutes.
4 Preheat grill. Uncover frittata; place pan (wrap handle in foil, if necessary) under heated grill about 5 minutes or until set and top is browned lightly. Stand in pan 5 minutes before serving.
preparation time *10 minutes*
cooking time *20 minutes* serves *4*
nutritional count per serving *38.1g total fat (19.6g saturated fat); 2190kJ (524 cal); 19g carbohydrate; 25.3g protein; 2.4g fibre*

angel hair frittata

spaghetti and meatballs

spaghetti napoletana

spaghetti and meatballs

Meatballs can be made and fried a day ahead; keep, covered, in the refrigerator until the sauce is made. If you like, double the meatball recipe and freeze half after frying. Thaw meatballs overnight in the refrigerator before adding to the sauce.

500g pork mince
2 tablespoons coarsely chopped fresh
    flat-leaf parsley
1 clove garlic, crushed
1 egg
1 cup (70g) stale breadcrumbs
1 tablespoon tomato paste
2 tablespoons olive oil
400g can crushed tomatoes
600ml bottled tomato pasta sauce
375g spaghetti
⅓ cup (25g) finely grated parmesan cheese

1 Combine pork, parsley, garlic, egg, breadcrumbs and paste in large bowl; roll tablespoons of pork mixture into balls. Heat oil in large saucepan; cook meatballs, in batches, until browned all over.
2 Place undrained tomatoes and sauce in same pan; bring to the boil. Return meatballs to pan, reduce heat; simmer, uncovered, about 10 minutes or until meatballs are cooked through.
3 Meanwhile, cook pasta in large saucepan of boiling water until tender; drain. Divide pasta among serving bowls; top with meatballs, sprinkle with cheese.
preparation time *15 minutes*
cooking time *20 minutes* serves *4*
nutritional count per serving *24.2g total fat*
(6.5g saturated fat); 3269kJ (782 cal);
89.1g carbohydrate; 46.6g protein; 8.7g fibre

spaghetti napoletana

2 x 400g cans chopped tomatoes
30g butter
1 tablespoon olive oil
2 cloves garlic, crushed
1 tablespoon finely shredded fresh basil
2 tablespoons finely chopped fresh
    flat-leaf parsley
250g spaghetti

1 Push tomatoes and their liquid through sieve.
2 Heat butter and oil in large saucepan, add garlic; cook, stirring, 1 minute. Add puréed tomato; bring to the boil. Reduce heat; simmer, uncovered, about 40 minutes or until sauce reduces by about half. Stir in basil and parsley.
3 Meanwhile, cook pasta in large saucepan of boiling water until tender; drain. Combine sauce and pasta.
preparation time *10 minutes*
cooking time *45 minutes* serves *2*
nutritional count per serving *23.7g total fat*
(9.7g saturated fat); 2913kJ (697 cal);
98.1g carbohydrate; 17.6g protein; 9.7g fibre

rigatoni with zucchini, lemon and mint

500g rigatoni pasta
¼ cup (60ml) olive oil
2 cloves garlic, crushed
3 medium zucchini (360g), grated coarsely
¾ cup (180g) ricotta cheese
1 cup coarsely chopped fresh mint
½ cup (70g) roasted slivered almonds
2 tablespoons lemon juice

1 Cook pasta in large saucepan of boiling water until tender; drain.
2 Meanwhile, heat oil in large frying pan; cook garlic and zucchini, stirring, 2 minutes. Add cheese; cook, stirring, until just heated through.
3 Combine zucchini mixture and pasta with remaining ingredients.
preparation time *10 minutes*
cooking time *10 minutes* serves *4*
nutritional count per serving *30.3g total fat (6g saturated fat); 3110kJ (744 cal); 88.9g carbohydrate; 23.9g protein; 8.3g fibre*

orecchiette boscaiola

375g orecchiette pasta
60g butter
2 rindless bacon rashers (130g),
   chopped finely
150g button mushrooms, sliced thinly
1 clove garlic, crushed
1 teaspoon cracked black pepper
300ml cream
½ cup (40g) finely grated parmesan cheese

1 Cook pasta in large saucepan of boiling water until tender; drain.
2 Meanwhile, melt butter in medium frying pan; cook bacon, stirring, 5 minutes. Add mushrooms and garlic; cook, stirring, 3 minutes.
3 Add pepper and cream; simmer, uncovered, about 5 minutes or until sauce reduces by half.
4 Add cheese; stir over low heat about 2 minutes or until cheese melts. Combine pasta and sauce in large bowl.

preparation time *10 minutes*
cooking time *10 minutes* serves *4*
nutritional count per serving *53.5g total fat (33.4g saturated fat); 3540kJ (847 cal); 66.6g carbohydrate; 23.6g protein; 4.3g fibre*

fettuccine with creamy tomato sausage sauce

3 Meanwhile, cook pasta in large saucepan of boiling water until tender; drain. Divide among serving bowls.
4 Stir sausage, onion and sage into tomato mixture; spoon sauce over pasta.
preparation time *10 minutes*
cooking time *30 minutes* serves *4*
nutritional count per serving *61.7g total fat (34.7g saturated fat); 4147kJ (992 cal); 74.8g carbohydrate; 29.6g protein; 6.8g fibre*

fettuccine with creamy tomato sausage sauce

Use thick pork sausages instead of the italian sausages, if you prefer.

cooking-oil spray
6 thick italian sausages (480g)
2 cloves garlic, crushed
400g can crushed tomatoes
¼ cup (60ml) dry white wine
300ml cream
375g fettuccine pasta
6 green onions, chopped finely
2 tablespoons fresh sage leaves

1 Lightly spray large frying pan with oil; cook sausages until browned all over and cooked through. Remove sausages from pan; chop coarsely. Cover to keep warm. Drain excess oil from pan.
2 Combine garlic, undrained tomatoes, wine and cream in same pan; bring to the boil. Reduce heat; simmer, uncovered, about 10 minutes or until sauce thickens slightly.

chilli and garlic spaghettini with breadcrumbs

Spaghettini is very thin spaghetti. You can use plain spaghetti instead of the spaghettini.

375g spaghettini
⅓ cup (80ml) olive oil
50g butter
4 cloves garlic, crushed
4 fresh small red chillies, seeded, chopped finely
2 cups (140g) stale breadcrumbs
½ cup coarsely chopped fresh flat-leaf parsley
2 teaspoons finely grated lemon rind

1 Cook pasta in large saucepan of boiling water until tender; drain.
2 Meanwhile, heat half the oil in large frying pan with butter until butter melts. Add garlic, chilli and breadcrumbs; cook, stirring, until breadcrumbs are browned lightly.
3 Combine pasta and breadcrumb mixture in large bowl with parsley, rind and remaining oil.
preparation time *10 minutes*
cooking time *10 minutes* serves *4*
nutritional count per serving *30.9g total fat (9.8g saturated fat); 2959kJ (708 cal); 88.4g carbohydrate; 15.9g protein; 5.6g fibre*

chilli and garlic spaghettini with breadcrumbs

fettuccine carbonara

Named for a pasta sauce made by Italian charcoal-makers, and easy enough to prepare that it could be whipped up in a single pot hung over the fire out in the forest, carbonara has come to represent the classic easy creamy pasta sauce.

4 rindless bacon rashers (260g), chopped coarsely
375g fettuccine pasta
3 egg yolks, beaten lightly
1 cup (250ml) cream
½ cup (30g) finely grated parmesan cheese
2 tablespoons coarsely chopped fresh chives

1 Cook pasta in large saucepan of boiling water until tender; drain.
2 Meanwhile, cook bacon in heated small frying pan, stirring, until crisp; drain.
3 Combine pasta in large bowl with egg yolks, cream, bacon and cheese; sprinkle with chives.

preparation time *10 minutes*
cooking time *10 minutes* serves *4*
nutritional count per serving *43.4g total fat (24.1g saturated fat); 3248kJ (777 cal); 66.1g carbohydrate; 29.5g protein; 3.1g fibre*

onion, anchovy and olive pizzetta

1 tablespoon olive oil

3 medium brown onions (450g), sliced thinly

2 tablespoons dry sherry, optional

4 x 112g pre-packaged pizza bases

2 tablespoons tomato paste

12 drained anchovy fillets, chopped coarsely

¼ cup (40g) thinly sliced seeded kalamata olives

2 tablespoons fresh oregano leaves

1 Preheat grill plate (or barbecue) to medium.

2 Meanwhile, heat oil in large frying pan; cook onion, stirring, until browned lightly. Add sherry; cook, stirring, until liquid evaporates.

3 Spread pizza bases with tomato paste. Divide onion mixture among bases; top with anchovies, olives and oregano. Cook, covered, over low heat about 5 minutes or until bases are heated through.

preparation time *15 minutes*

cooking time *20 minutes*   serves *4*

nutritional count per serving   *10.1g total fat (1.5g saturated fat); 1889kJ (452 cal); 68.9g carbohydrate; 15.1g protein; 6.2g fibre*

potato, garlic and oregano pizza

potato, garlic and oregano pizza

You can use pre-packaged pizza bases for this recipe, if you prefer.

2 teaspoons dried yeast
½ teaspoon caster sugar
¾ cup (180ml) warm water
2 cups (300g) plain flour
1 teaspoon salt
2 tablespoons olive oil
2 tablespoons polenta
⅓ cup loosely packed fresh oregano leaves
6 small potatoes (720g), sliced thinly
3 cloves garlic, crushed
2 tablespoons olive oil, extra
½ teaspoon sea salt flakes
1 tablespoon fresh oregano leaves, extra

1 Combine yeast, sugar and the water in small bowl, cover; stand in warm place about 10 minutes or until mixture is frothy.
2 Sift flour and salt into large bowl; stir in yeast mixture and oil. Mix to a soft dough. Bring dough together with hands, adding extra water if necessary.
3 Knead dough on floured surface about 10 minutes or until smooth and elastic. Place in oiled bowl, cover; stand in warm place 1 hour or until doubled in size.
4 Preheat oven to 240°C/220°C fan-forced. Lightly oil two oven trays.
5 Punch dough down with fist; knead on floured surface until smooth. Divide dough in half; roll halves into 20cm x 30cm rectangles; place on trays. Sprinkle dough with polenta; prick with fork.
6 Divide oregano leaves between bases then layer with potato, overlapping slightly. Brush combined garlic and extra oil over potato.
7 Bake about 20 minutes or until potato is tender and bases are crisp. Sprinkle pizzas with sea salt and extra oregano before serving.

preparation time *25 minutes (plus standing time)*
cooking time *20 minutes* serves *4*
nutritional count per serving *19.5g total fat (2.8g saturated fat); 2328kJ (557 cal); 79.1g carbohydrate; 12.8g protein; 6.1g fibre*

pizza caprese

pizza caprese

We used large (25cm diameter) packaged pizza bases for this recipe.

2 x 335g pizza bases
½ cup (140g) tomato paste
4 large egg tomatoes (360g), sliced thinly
210g bocconcini cheese, halved
¼ cup finely shredded fresh basil

1 Preheat oven to 220°C/200°C fan-forced. Oil two oven trays.
2 Spread bases with paste; top with tomato and cheese. Cook, uncovered, about 15 minutes. Sprinkle pizzas with basil.

preparation time *10 minutes*
cooking time *15 minutes* serves *4*
nutritional count per serving *14.6g total fat (6.1g saturated fat); 2658kJ (636 cal); 94.5g carbohydrate; 26.1g protein; 9g fibre*

turkish herbed lamb pizza

You can use pre-packaged pizza bases for this recipe, if you prefer.

¾ teaspoon dried yeast
1 teaspoon white sugar
¾ cup (180ml) warm water
2 cups (300g) plain flour
1 teaspoon salt
cooking-oil spray
600g lamb mince
1 tablespoon olive oil
1 small brown onion (80g), chopped finely
1 clove garlic, crushed
½ teaspoon ground cinnamon
1½ teaspoons ground allspice
¼ cup (40g) pine nuts, chopped coarsely
¼ cup (70g) tomato paste
2 medium tomatoes (300g), seeded, chopped finely
1 cup (250ml) chicken stock
2 tablespoons lemon juice
¼ cup finely chopped fresh flat-leaf parsley
¼ cup finely chopped fresh mint
½ cup (140g) greek-style yogurt
2 tablespoons cold water

1 Whisk yeast, sugar and the warm water in small bowl; cover, stand in warm place about 15 minutes or until mixture is frothy.
2 Combine flour and salt in large bowl; stir in yeast mixture, mix to a soft dough. Knead on lightly floured surface about 10 minutes or until smooth and elastic. Place in large oiled bowl, turning dough once to coat in oil. Cover dough; stand in warm place about 1 hour or until dough is doubled in size.
3 Halve dough; knead each portion until smooth then roll out to oval shape measuring approximately 12cm x 35cm. Place each oval on a lightly oiled oven tray; spray lightly with cooking-oil spray. Cover; stand in warm place 30 minutes.
4 Preheat oven to 240°C/220°C fan-forced.
5 Cook mince in heated oiled large frying pan, stirring, until cooked through; place in medium bowl.
6 Heat oil in same pan; cook onion and garlic, stirring, until onion softens. Add spices and nuts; cook, stirring, about 5 minutes or until nuts are just toasted. Return mince to pan with tomato paste, tomato, stock and juice; cook, stirring, about 5 minutes or until liquid is almost evaporated. Remove pan from heat; stir in herbs.
7 Spoon mince mixture over pizza bases; cook, uncovered, in oven, about 15 minutes or until bases are cooked through and tops are browned lightly. Serve drizzled with combined yogurt and the cold water.
preparation time *45 minutes (plus standing time)*
cooking time *35 minutes* serves *4*
nutritional count per serving *26.5g total fat (7.7g saturated fat); 2805kJ (671 cal); 63g carbohydrate; 44.2g protein; 5.3g fibre*

mushroom, olive & anchovy pizza

We used a large (25cm diameter) thick-based packaged pizza base for this recipe.
Pizza can be prepared and frozen in its unbaked form. Place frozen pizza in hot oven; allow about 10 minutes extra cooking time.

2 teaspoons olive oil
1 medium brown onion (150g), chopped finely
1 clove garlic, crushed
410g can crushed tomatoes
1 tablespoon tomato paste
2 teaspoons finely chopped fresh oregano
1 teaspoon white sugar
1 x 335g pizza base
1¼ cups (125g) grated mozzarella cheese
2 tablespoons grated parmesan cheese
45g can anchovy fillets, drained
1 small red capsicum (150g), sliced thinly
3 button mushrooms, sliced thinly
½ cup (60g) seeded black olives, halved
¼ cup loosely packed fresh basil leaves

1 Heat oil in large saucepan; cook onion until soft. Add garlic; stir 1 minute. Add undrained tomatoes, paste, oregano and sugar; bring to the boil. Reduce heat; simmer, uncovered, stirring occasionally, about 10 minutes or until sauce is thick and smooth; cool.
2 Preheat oven to 220°C/200°C fan-forced.
3 Spread cooled sauce over base of pizza.
4 Combine cheeses in small bowl; sprinkle half the cheese over pizza, top with anchovies, capsicum and mushrooms. Sprinkle with olives and remaining cheese. Bake about 15 minutes or until crust is golden brown. Sprinkle with basil.

preparation time *10 minutes (plus cooling time)*
cooking time *35 minutes* serves *4*
nutritional count per serving *14.4g total fat (6g saturated fat); 1889kJ (452 cal); 55.8 carbohydrate; 21.5g protein; 6g fibre*

potatoes & other vegies

baked potatoes

The perfect baked potato should be salty and crisp on the outside and snow white and fluffy on the inside. You can also use russet burbank or spunta potatoes for this recipe.

8 king edward potatoes (1.4kg), unpeeled

1 Preheat oven to 180°C/160°C fan-forced.
2 Pierce skin of each potato with fork; wrap each potato in foil, place on oven tray. Bake about 1 hour or until tender. Top with topping of your choice.
preparation time *5 minutes*
cooking time *1 hour* makes *8*
nutritional count per potato *0.2g total fat (0g saturated fat); 493kJ (118 cal); 22.9g carbohydrate; 4.2g protein; 3.5g fibre*

toppings

Each topping is enough for eight potatoes.
preparation time *5 minutes*

cream cheese and pesto
Combine ⅔ cup spreadable cream cheese, ⅓ cup pesto and ½ teaspoon cracked black pepper in small bowl; refrigerate until required.
nutritional count per potato *11.3g total fat (5.2g saturated fat); 966kJ (231 cal); 23.6g carbohydrate; 7g protein; 3.8g fibre*

lime and chilli yogurt
Combine ⅔ cup yogurt, 2 tablespoons coarsely chopped fresh coriander, 2 finely chopped fresh small red thai chillies and 1 teaspoon finely grated lime rind in small bowl; refrigerate until required.
nutritional count per potato *1g total fat (0.5g saturated fat); 564kJ (135 cal); 24.1g carbohydrate; 5.3g protein; 3.5g fibre*

mustard and walnut butter
Mash 60g softened butter, 1 teaspoon wholegrain mustard and 2 tablespoons finely chopped toasted walnuts in small bowl until mixture forms a paste; refrigerate until required.
nutritional count per potato *7.9g total fat (4.1g saturated fat); 790kJ (189 cal); 23.1g carbohydrate; 4.6g protein; 3.7g fibre*

potato cakes

potato cakes

The combination of mashed potato, bacon, onion, cheese and sour cream in these cakes is so good you'll find it hard to stop at one. You can also use lasoda or pink-eye potatoes for this recipe.

1kg sebago potatoes, chopped coarsely
4 green onions, sliced thinly
4 rindless bacon rashers (260g), chopped finely
⅓ cup (40g) coarsely grated cheddar cheese
2 tablespoons sour cream
½ cup (75g) plain flour
50g butter
2 tablespoons olive oil

1 Boil, steam or microwave potato until tender; drain. Mash potato in large bowl until smooth.
2 Meanwhile, cook onion and bacon in heated oiled large frying pan, stirring, until bacon is crisp. Add bacon mixture to potato with cheese and sour cream; stir to combine. Shape potato mixture into 12 patties; toss in flour, shake off excess.
3 Heat butter and oil in same pan; cook potato cakes, in batches, until browned lightly both sides.
preparation time *15 minutes*
cooking time *30 minutes* makes *12*
nutritional count per cake *11.9g total fat (5.3g saturated fat); 823kJ (197 cal); 14.1g carbohydrate; 7.6g protein; 1.4g fibre*

mixed dhal

The word 'dhal' is the Hindi word for legumes and pulses; regarded as meat substitutes, they feature widely in Indian cooking because they are a good source of protein for this largely vegetarian nation.

2 tablespoons ghee
1 medium brown onion (150g), chopped finely
2 cloves garlic, crushed
4cm piece fresh ginger (20g), grated
1½ tablespoons black mustard seeds
1 long green chilli, chopped finely
1 tablespoon ground cumin
1 tablespoon ground coriander
2 teaspoons ground turmeric
½ cup (100g) brown lentils
⅓ cup (65g) red lentils
⅓ cup (85g) yellow split peas
⅓ cup (85g) green split peas
400g can crushed tomatoes
2 cups (500ml) vegetable stock
1½ cups (375ml) water
140ml can coconut cream

1 Heat ghee in large saucepan; cook onion, garlic and ginger, stirring, until onion softens. Add seeds, chilli and spices; cook, stirring, until fragrant.
2 Add lentils and peas to pan. Stir in undrained tomatoes, stock and the water; simmer, covered, stirring occasionally, about 1 hour or until lentils are tender.
3 Just before serving, add coconut cream; stir over low heat until curry is heated through.
preparation time *15 minutes*
cooking time *1 hour 10 minutes* serves *4*
nutritional count per serving *18.4g total fat (12.5g saturated fat); 1898kJ (454 cal); 42.6g carbohydrate; 23.3g protein; 12.7g fibre*

mixed dhal

cauliflower and green pea curry

Cauliflower is a popular choice for vegetarian curries because it's both filling and, while it has a great taste of its own, the texture of the florets captures the sauce. In this recipe we used vindaloo paste, but any hot curry paste (red curry paste, for example) would work just as well. Or, if you prefer, use a curry paste that suits your heat-tolerance level.

600g cauliflower florets
2 tablespoons ghee
1 medium brown onion (150g), chopped finely
2 cloves garlic, crushed
2cm piece fresh ginger (10g), grated
¼ cup (75g) hot curry paste
¾ cup (180ml) cream
2 large tomatoes (440g), chopped coarsely
1 cup (120g) frozen peas
1 cup (280g) yogurt
3 hard-boiled eggs, sliced thinly
¼ cup finely chopped fresh coriander

1 Boil, steam or microwave cauliflower until just tender; drain.
2 Meanwhile, heat ghee in large saucepan; cook onion, garlic and ginger, stirring, until onion softens. Add paste; cook, stirring, until mixture is fragrant.
3 Add cream to pan; bring to the boil then reduce heat. Add cauliflower and tomato; simmer, uncovered, 5 minutes, stirring occasionally.
4 Add peas and yogurt to pan; stir over low heat about 5 minutes or until peas are just cooked. Serve curry sprinkled with egg and coriander.
preparation time *20 minutes*
cooking time *30 minutes* serves *4*
nutritional count per serving *40.9g total fat (21.9g saturated fat); 2132kJ (510 cal); 15.5g carbohydrate; 17g protein; 8.6g fibre*

portuguese potatoes

Piri-piri is a Portuguese hot sauce made of chilli, garlic, ginger, oil and herbs, and is available from supermarkets. You can also use pontiac potatoes for this recipe.

600g sebago potatoes, chopped coarsely
2 tablespoons olive oil
2 cloves garlic, crushed
1 large brown onion (200g), chopped coarsely
4 medium tomatoes (600g), chopped coarsely
2 teaspoons sweet paprika
2 teaspoons finely chopped fresh thyme
½ cup (125ml) chicken stock
1 tablespoon piri-piri sauce
1 tablespoon coarsely chopped fresh
   flat-leaf parsley

1 Preheat oven to 220°C/200°C fan-forced.
2 Toss potato and half the oil in medium shallow baking dish. Roast, uncovered, about 30 minutes or until browned lightly.
3 Meanwhile, heat remaining oil in large frying pan; cook garlic and onion, stirring, until onion softens. Add tomato, paprika and thyme; cook, stirring, about 1 minute or until tomato just softens. Add stock and sauce; bring to the boil. Reduce heat; simmer, uncovered, stirring occasionally, about 10 minutes or until sauce thickens slightly.
4 Remove potato from oven; reduce oven temperature to 180°C/160°C fan-forced.
5 Pour sauce over potato; bake, uncovered, about 20 minutes or until potato is tender. Serve sprinkled with parsley.

preparation time *15 minutes*
cooking time *50 minutes* serves *6*
nutritional count per serving *6.5g total fat (0.9g saturated fat); 602kJ (144 cal); 15.7g carbohydrate; 4g protein; 3.6g fibre*

potatoes byron

potatoes byron

You can also use pink-eye or sebago potatoes for this recipe.

1kg russet burbank potatoes, unpeeled
60g butter, chopped
½ cup (125ml) cream
¼ cup (20g) finely grated parmesan cheese
¼ cup (30g) finely grated gruyère cheese

1 Preheat oven to 180°C/160°C fan-forced. Oil four shallow 1-cup (250ml) ovenproof dishes.
2 Pierce skin of each potato with fork; place on oven tray. Bake, uncovered, about 1 hour or until tender. Cover; cool 10 minutes.
3 Split potatoes in half lengthways; scoop flesh into medium bowl, discard potato skins. Mash potato with butter.
4 Lightly divide potato among prepared dishes. Pour cream evenly over potato; sprinkle with combined cheeses. Bake, uncovered, in oven, about 10 minutes or until heated through and browned lightly.

preparation time *10 minutes*
cooking time *1 hour 10 minutes* serves *4*
nutritional count per serving *30.2g total fat (19.7g saturated fat); 1910kJ (457 cal); 33.8g carbohydrate; 10.8g protein; 5g fibre*

spanish tortilla

You can also use bintje or pink fir apple potatoes for this recipe.
Chorizo is a sausage of Spanish origin, made of coarsely ground pork and highly seasoned with garlic and chillies. Use your favourite spicy sausage in this dish, if you prefer.

800g russet burbank potatoes, sliced thinly
1 tablespoon olive oil
1 large brown onion (200g), sliced thinly
200g chorizo sausage, sliced thinly
6 eggs, beaten lightly
300ml cream
4 green onions, sliced thickly
¼ cup (25g) coarsely grated mozzarella cheese
¼ cup (30g) coarsely grated cheddar cheese

1 Boil, steam or microwave potato until just tender; drain.
2 Meanwhile, heat oil in medium frying pan; cook brown onion, stirring, until softened. Add chorizo; cook, stirring, until crisp. Drain chorizo mixture on absorbent paper; slice thinly.
3 Whisk eggs in large bowl with cream, green onion and cheeses; stir in potato and chorizo mixture.
4 Pour mixture into heated oiled medium frying pan; cook, covered, over low heat about 10 minutes or until tortilla is just set. Carefully invert tortilla onto plate, then slide back into pan; cook, uncovered, about 5 minutes or until cooked through.

preparation time *15 minutes*
cooking time *30 minutes* serves *4*
nutritional count per serving *64.1g total fat (32g saturated fat); 3390kJ (811 cal); 29.1g carbohydrate; 29.5g protein; 3.8g fibre*

spanish tortilla

banana chillies with potato and green olive stuffing

We used banana chillies, also known as hungarian or sweet banana peppers. They are almost as mild as capsicums, but possess a slightly sweet sharp taste. They can be pale olive green, yellow and red in colour, and are available from supermarkets.

40g butter
2 tablespoons olive oil
3 cloves garlic, crushed
2 teaspoons ground cumin
2 teaspoons dried oregano
600g potatoes, diced into 1cm pieces
3 large tomatoes (660g), diced into 1cm pieces
1 cup (120g) seeded green olives,
    chopped coarsely
2 cups (240g) coarsely grated cheddar cheese
8 red or yellow banana chillies (1kg)
tomato sauce
1 tablespoon olive oil
1 clove garlic, crushed
1 medium red onion (170g), chopped coarsely
1 tablespoon ground cumin
2 teaspoons dried oregano
2 x 425g cans diced tomatoes
½ cup (125ml) water

1 Preheat oven to 180°C/160°C fan-forced.
2 Heat butter and oil in frying pan; cook garlic, cumin, oregano and potato about 10 minutes or until potato browns lightly. Add tomato and olives; cook, stirring, about 10 minutes or until liquid has evaporated. Transfer to large bowl; stir in cheese.
3 Meanwhile, using sharp knife, make a small horizontal cut in one chilli 1cm below stem, then make a lengthways slit in chilli, starting from horizontal cut and ending 1cm from the tip, taking care not to cut all the way through chilli; discard membrane and seeds. Repeat process with remaining chillies. Carefully divide filling among chillies, securing each closed with a toothpick.
4 Make tomato sauce. Place chillies on tomato sauce in dish, cover; cook in oven about 40 minutes or until chillies are tender. Serve chillies with tomato sauce and a mixed green salad, if desired.

tomato sauce Heat oil in large deep flameproof baking dish; cook garlic, onion, cumin and oregano, stirring, until onion softens. Add undrained tomatoes and the water; bring to the boil. Reduce heat; simmer, uncovered, 10 minutes.

preparation time *50 minutes*
cooking time *1 hour 10 minutes* serves *4*
nutritional count per serving *43.8g total fat (20.3g saturated fat); 2725kJ (652 cal); 39.9g carbohydrate; 24.4g protein; 11.2g fibre*

chickpea vegetable braise with cumin couscous

1 cup (200g) dried chickpeas
2 tablespoons olive oil
2 small leeks (400g), chopped coarsely
2 medium carrots (240g), cut into batons
2 cloves garlic, crushed
1 tablespoon finely chopped fresh rosemary
2 tablespoons white wine vinegar
2 cups (500ml) vegetable stock
100g baby spinach leaves
¼ cup (60ml) lemon juice
2 tablespoons olive oil, extra
2 cloves garlic, crushed, extra
cumin couscous
1 cup (250ml) boiling water
1 cup (200g) couscous
1 tablespoon olive oil
1 teaspoon ground cumin

1 Place chickpeas in medium bowl, cover with cold water; stand overnight, drain. Rinse under cold water; drain. Place chickpeas in medium saucepan of boiling water. Return to the boil, reduce heat; simmer, uncovered, about 40 minutes or until chickpeas are tender. Drain.

2 Meanwhile, preheat oven to 160°C/140°C fan-forced.

3 Heat oil in large deep flameproof baking dish; cook leek and carrot, stirring, until just tender. Add garlic, rosemary and chickpeas; cook, stirring, until fragrant. Add vinegar and stock; bring to the boil. Cover; cook in oven 30 minutes.

4 Meanwhile, make cumin couscous. Make tomato and red onion salad.

5 Remove dish from oven; stir in spinach, juice, extra oil and extra garlic. Serve chickpea vegetable braise with couscous and tomato and red onion salad.

cumin couscous Combine the water and couscous in medium heatproof bowl, cover; stand 5 minutes or until liquid is absorbed, fluffing with fork occasionally. Add oil and cumin; toss gently to combine.

preparation time *20 minutes (plus standing time)* cooking time *1 hour 25 minutes* serves *4* nutritional count per serving *26.9g total fat (3.9g saturated fat); 2483kJ (594 cal); 63.2g carbohydrate; 19.0g protein; 11.4g fibre*

basil butter kumara patties with tomato and bean salad

2 medium kumara (800g), chopped coarsely
40g butter, softened
⅓ cup finely chopped fresh basil
¼ cup (40g) roasted pine nuts
1 clove garlic, crushed
2 tablespoons coarsely grated parmesan cheese
½ cup (35g) stale wholemeal breadcrumbs
2 tablespoons olive oil

1 Boil, steam or microwave kumara until tender; drain.
2 Mash kumara with butter in medium bowl; stir in basil, nuts, garlic, cheese and breadcrumbs. When cool enough to handle, shape kumara mixture into eight patties.
3 Heat oil in large frying pan; cook patties, in two batches, until browned both sides and heated through.
4 Meanwhile, make tomato and bean salad. Serve patties with salad.

preparation time *15 minutes*
cooking time *30 minutes* serves *4*
nutritional count per serving *37g total fat (11.7g saturated fat); 2324kJ (555 cal); 35.8g carbohydrate; 15.8g protein; 10g fibre*

tomato and bean salad

1 small green oak leaf lettuce, leaves torn
425g can white beans, rinsed drained
250g cherry tomatoes, halved
½ cup (100g) crumbled fetta cheese
½ cup loosely packed fresh basil leaves
1 tablespoon olive oil
1 tablespoon white wine vinegar
1 teaspoon dijon mustard

1 Combine ingredients in large bowl.

chickpeas in spicy tomato sauce

This recipe gets its heat from the cayenne, the ground dried pods of a special variety of pungent chilli. Serve with raita, and Indian breads such as chapati, poori or paratha.

2 tablespoons ghee
2 teaspoons cumin seeds
2 medium brown onions (300g), chopped finely
2 cloves garlic, crushed
4cm piece fresh ginger (20g), grated
1 tablespoon ground coriander
1 teaspoon ground turmeric
1 teaspoon cayenne pepper
2 tablespoons tomato paste
2 x 400g cans diced tomatoes
2 cups (500ml) water
2 x 420g cans chickpeas, rinsed, drained
1 large kumara (500g), cut into 1.5cm pieces
300g spinach, trimmed, chopped coarsely

1 Heat ghee in large saucepan; cook seeds, stirring, until fragrant. Add onion, garlic and ginger; cook, stirring, until onion softens. Add spices; cook, stirring, until fragrant. Add tomato paste; cook, stirring, 2 minutes.
2 Add undrained tomatoes, the water, chickpeas and kumara to pan; simmer, covered, stirring occasionally, about 30 minutes or until kumara is tender and mixture thickens slightly.
3 Stir in spinach just before serving.
preparation time *15 minutes*
cooking time *45 minutes* serves 6
nutritional count per serving *8.1g total fat (4.1g saturated fat); 1037kJ (248 cal); 29.1g carbohydrate; 9.9g protein; 9.4g fibre*

spinach and corn pasties

1 tablespoon vegetable oil

2 medium potatoes (400g), diced into 1cm pieces

1 small brown onion (80g), chopped finely

250g frozen spinach, thawed, drained

2 x 310g cans creamed corn

3 sheets ready-rolled shortcrust pastry

2 tablespoons milk

1 Heat half the oil in large frying pan; cook potato, stirring, until browned lightly. Add onion; cook, stirring, until soft. Combine potato, onion, spinach and corn in large bowl.

2 Preheat oven to 200°C/180°C fan-forced. Oil two oven trays.

3 Cut pastry sheets in half diagonally. Divide filling among triangles, placing on one side; fold pastry in half to enclose filling, pressing edges with fork to seal.

4 Place pasties on trays; brush with milk. Bake about 30 minutes or until browned lightly. Serve with sweet chilli sauce, if desired.

preparation time *20 minutes*

cooking time *45 minutes* makes *6*

nutritional count per pastie *27.1g total fat (12.6g saturated fat); 2291kJ (548 cal); 62.7g carbohydrate; 9.8g protein; 7.5g fibre*

tofu and vegetable curry

This vegetable recipe is a good example of a typical Thai curry from the south of the country where the food bears the closest similarities to the food of India. The chilli, turmeric, ginger and coconut milk could just as easily be found in a southern Indian vegetable curry as they are in this.

300g firm silken tofu
6 cloves garlic, quartered
3 fresh small red thai chillies, chopped coarsely
10cm stick (20g) fresh lemon grass,
    chopped coarsely
1.5cm piece fresh turmeric (20g), chopped coarsely
4cm piece fresh ginger (20g), chopped coarsely
1 medium brown onion (150g), chopped finely
1 tablespoon vegetable oil
400ml can coconut milk
1 cup (250ml) vegetable stock
2 fresh kaffir lime leaves
4 medium zucchini (480g), chopped coarsely
1 small cauliflower (1kg), cut into florets
1 tablespoon light soy sauce
1 tablespoon lime juice
⅓ cup firmly packed fresh coriander,
    chopped coarsely
¼ cup loosely packed thai basil leaves

1 Press tofu between two chopping boards with a weight on top, raise one end; stand 10 minutes. Cut tofu into 2cm cubes; pat dry between layers of absorbent paper.
2 Blend or process garlic, chilli, lemon grass, turmeric, ginger, onion and oil until mixture forms a paste.
3 Cook garlic paste in large saucepan, stirring, 5 minutes. Add coconut milk, stock and lime leaves; simmer, uncovered, stirring occasionally, 10 minutes.
4 Add zucchini and cauliflower; simmer, uncovered, about 5 minutes or until vegetables are tender.
5 Discard lime leaves; stir in tofu, sauce, juice and coriander. Sprinkle with basil before serving.
preparation time *25 minutes*
cooking time *25 minutes* serves *4*
nutritional count per serving *31.7g total fat (19.7g saturated fat); 1843kJ (441 cal); 14.8g carbohydrate; 19.8g protein; 11g fibre*

canned & fresh fish

salmon and green bean potato patties

We used sebago potatoes in this recipe; you can also use lasoda, coliban, nicola or pink-eye.

150g green beans
800g potatoes, chopped coarsely
20g butter
⅓ cup (25g) finely grated parmesan cheese
1 egg
415g can red salmon
⅓ cup (35g) packaged breadcrumbs
vegetable oil, for shallow-frying
150g baby spinach leaves
1 medium lemon (140g), cut into wedges

1 Boil, steam or microwave beans until tender; drain. Rinse under cold water; drain, chop coarsely.
2 Boil, steam or microwave potato until tender; drain. Mash potato in large bowl with butter, cheese and egg until smooth.
3 Drain salmon; discard skin and bones. Add salmon and beans to potato mixture; mix well. Shape salmon mixture into 12 patties; coat in breadcrumbs. Place patties on tray, cover; refrigerate 30 minutes.
4 Heat oil in large frying pan; shallow-fry patties, in batches, until browned lightly and heated through. Drain on absorbent paper; serve on baby spinach leaves with lemon wedges.

preparation time *20 minutes
(plus refrigeration time)*
cooking time *30 minutes* serves *4*
nutritional count per serving *51.7g total fat
(8.7g saturated fat); 2959kJ (708 cal);
29.6g carbohydrate; 29.5g protein; 5.6g fibre*

perfect salmon patties

1 Boil, steam or microwave potatoes until tender; drain. Mash potato in large bowl.

2 Drain salmon; discard any skin and bones. Add salmon to potato with onion, parsley, rind and juice; mix well. Cover; refrigerate 30 minutes.

3 Using floured hands, shape salmon mixture into eight patties. Toss patties in flour; shake away excess. Dip patties, one at a time, in combined egg and milk, then in combined breadcrumbs.

4 Heat oil in large saucepan; deep-fry patties, in batches, until browned lightly. Drain on absorbent paper. Serve with a salad.

preparation time *20 minutes (plus refrigeration time)*
cooking time *20 minutes* makes *8*
nutritional count per pattie *16.7g total fat (3.6g saturated fat); 1396kJ (334 cal); 28.6g carbohydrate; 15.9g protein; 2.7g fibre*

perfect salmon patties

Salmon patties are quite easy to make as all the necessary ingredients can usually be found in your pantry. Patties can be prepared a day ahead and refrigerated, covered. You can also use coliban or nicola potatoes for this recipe.

1kg lasoda potatoes
440g can red salmon
1 small brown onion (80g), chopped finely
1 tablespoon finely chopped fresh flat-leaf parsley
1 teaspoon finely grated lemon rind
1 tablespoon lemon juice
½ cup (75g) plain flour
1 egg
2 tablespoons milk
½ cup (50g) packaged breadcrumbs
½ cup (35g) stale breadcrumbs
vegetable oil, for deep-frying

tuna and cannellini bean salad

2 cups (400g) dried cannellini beans
425g can tuna in springwater, drained
1 small red onion (100g), sliced thinly
2 stalks celery (300g), trimmed, sliced thinly
italian dressing
⅓ cup (80ml) olive oil
⅓ cup (80ml) lemon juice
1 tablespoon finely chopped fresh oregano
2 cloves garlic, crushed

1 Place beans in medium bowl, cover with cold water; stand overnight, drain. Rinse under cold water; drain. Place beans in medium saucepan of boiling water; return to the boil. Reduce heat; simmer, uncovered, about 1 hour or until beans are almost tender. Drain.

2 Meanwhile, make italian dressing.

3 Combine beans and dressing in large bowl with tuna, onion and celery.

italian dressing Combine ingredients in screw-top jar; shake well.

preparation time *10 minutes (plus standing time)*
cooking time *1 hour* serves *4*
nutritional count per serving *21.6g total fat (3.8g saturated fat); 1651kJ (395 cal); 17.3g carbohydrate; 28.8g protein; 8.5g fibre*

tuna and cannellini bean salad

tuna mornay

30g butter
1 medium brown onion (150g), chopped finely
1 stalk celery (150g), trimmed, chopped finely
1 tablespoon plain flour
¾ cup (180ml) milk
½ cup (125ml) cream
⅓ cup (40g) grated cheddar cheese
130g can corn kernels, rinsed, drained
2 x 185g can tuna, drained
1 cup (70g) stale breadcrumbs
¼ cup (30g) grated cheddar cheese, extra

1 Preheat oven to 180°C/160°C fan-forced.
2 Melt butter in medium saucepan; cook onion and celery, stirring, until onion is soft. Add flour; cook, stirring, 1 minute. Gradually stir in combined milk and cream; cook, stirring, until mixture boils and thickens. Remove pan from heat, add cheese, corn and tuna; stir until cheese is melted.
3 Spoon mornay mixture into four 1½-cup (375ml) ovenproof dishes. Sprinkle mornay with combined breadcrumbs and extra cheese.
4 Bake mornay, in oven, about 15 minutes or until heated through.

preparation time *5 minutes*
cooking time *25 minutes* serves *4*
nutritional count per serving *30.2g total fat (18.8g saturated fat); 2031kJ (486 cal); 23.4g carbohydrate; 29.3g protein; 2.5g fibre*

tuna spinach mornay pie with mash

50g butter

1 medium brown onion (150g), sliced thinly

¼ cup (35g) plain flour

2 cups (500ml) milk, warmed

150g baby spinach leaves

425g can tuna in springwater, drained

2 tablespoons lemon juice

potato and celeriac mash

400g potatoes, chopped coarsely

300g celeriac, chopped coarsely

2 tablespoons milk

30g butter

¼ cup (20g) finely grated parmesan cheese

1 Make potato and celeriac mash.

2 Melt butter in medium saucepan; cook onion, stirring, about 5 minutes or until softened. Add flour; cook, stirring, until mixture thickens and bubbles. Gradually add milk; stir until mixture boils and thickens. Remove from heat; stir in spinach, tuna and juice.

3 Preheat grill.

4 Spoon tuna mixture into shallow flameproof 1.5-litre (6-cup) dish; top with mash. Grill until browned lightly.

potato and celeriac mash Boil, steam or microwave potato and celeriac, separately, until tender; drain. Combine potato and celeriac in large bowl; mash with milk and butter until smooth. Stir in cheese; cover to keep warm.

preparation time *20 minutes*

cooking time *30 minutes* serves *4*

nutritional count per serving *25.8g total fat (12.1g saturated fat); 2040kJ (488 cal); 29.7g carbohydrate; 31.7g protein; 5.8g fibre*

smoked fish pot pies

3 Melt extra butter in medium saucepan; cook onion and garlic, stirring, until onion softens. Add flour; cook, stirring, until mixture thickens and bubbles. Gradually add extra milk; stir until mixture boils and thickens. Add peas, rind and juice; remove from heat. Stir in fish.
4 Preheat grill.
5 Divide egg, fish mixture and potato mixture among four 2-cup (500ml) flameproof dishes. Place dishes on oven tray; grill until tops are browned lightly.
preparation time *30 minutes*
cooking time *35 minutes* serves *4*
nutritional count per serving *30.2g total fat (17.9g saturated fat); 3160kJ (756 cal); 53.4g carbohydrate; 64g protein; 6.3g fibre*

smoked fish pot pies

You can also use lasoda or nicola potatoes for this recipe.

750g smoked cod fillets
2 cups (500ml) milk
1 bay leaf
6 black peppercorns
1kg coliban potatoes, chopped coarsely
50g butter, softened
20g butter, extra
1 large brown onion (200g), chopped finely
1 clove garlic, crushed
¼ cup (35g) plain flour
2½ cups (625ml) milk, extra
1 cup (120g) frozen peas
1 teaspoon finely grated lemon rind
2 tablespoons lemon juice
2 hard-boiled eggs, quartered

1 Place fish, milk, bay leaf and peppercorns in medium saucepan; bring to the boil. Reduce heat; simmer, uncovered, 10 minutes. Drain; discard liquid, bay leaf and peppercorns. When cool enough to handle, remove and discard skin from fish: flake flesh into large chunks into medium bowl.
2 Meanwhile, boil, steam or microwave potato until tender; drain. Mash potato with softened butter in large bowl until smooth; cover to keep warm.

white fish brandade

While a classic French brandade is a purée based on salted cod, olive oil, milk and garlic, it can be made with any fish. We used ling here, and the resultant take on the traditional is not only just as good but easier to prepare, too. Serve it as a dip with crusty bread.

200g sebago potatoes, chopped coarsely
2 cups (500ml) milk
350g white fish fillets, skin removed
1 small white onion (80g), chopped coarsely
2 cloves garlic, quartered
2 tablespoons olive oil
2 tablespoons lemon juice
¼ cup (60g) sour cream

1 Boil, steam or microwave potato until tender; drain.
2 Meanwhile, bring milk to the boil in large frying pan; add fish, return to the boil, then simmer, uncovered, until fish is cooked through, turning once.
3 When fish is cool enough to handle, break up over food processor or blender; process with cooled potato and remaining ingredients until mixture forms a smooth paste. Place brandade in serving bowl; cover and refrigerate 30 minutes.
preparation time *15 minutes (plus refrigeration time)*
cooking time *10 minutes* makes *2 cups*
nutritional count per tablespoon *3.7g total fat (1.5g saturated fat); 242kJ (58 cal); 2.3g carbohydrate; 4g protein; 0.2g fibre*

white fish brandade

mince

gourmet beef burgers

750g beef mince
1 cup (70g) stale breadcrumbs
2 tablespoons finely chopped fresh
    flat-leaf parsley
2 tablespoons sun-dried tomato paste
125g mozzarella cheese, thinly sliced
½ cup (150g) mayonnaise
4 bread rolls
50g mesclun
1 small red onion (100g), thinly sliced
2 tablespoons drained, sliced sun-dried
    tomatoes in oil

1 Combine mince, breadcrumbs, parsley and
1½ tablespoons of the paste in large bowl. Shape
mixture into four patties.
2 Cook patties on heated oiled barbecue,
uncovered, until browned and cooked through.
Top patties with cheese; cook until cheese melts.
3 Combine remaining paste and mayonnaise in
small bowl.
4 Split rolls in half. Place each half, cut-side down,
onto barbecue; cook until lightly toasted.
5 Sandwich patties, mayonnaise mixture,
mesclun, onion and sliced tomatoes between
bread rolls.
preparation time *15 minutes*
cooking time *10 minutes* serves *4*
nutritional count per serving *35g total fat
(11.6g saturated fat); 3118kJ (746 cal);
50.4g carbohydrate; 55.6g protein; 4.7g fibre*

beef, tomato and pea pies

1 tablespoon vegetable oil
1 small brown onion (80g), chopped finely
300g beef mince
400g can crushed tomatoes
1 tablespoon tomato paste
2 tablespoons worcestershire sauce
½ cup (125ml) beef stock
½ cup (60g) frozen peas
3 sheets ready-rolled puff pastry
1 egg, beaten lightly

1 Heat oil in large saucepan; cook onion, stirring, until softened. Add mince; cook, stirring, until changed in colour. Stir in undrained tomatoes, paste, sauce and stock; bring to the boil. Reduce heat; simmer, uncovered, about 20 minutes or until sauce thickens. Stir in peas. Cool.
2 Preheat oven to 200°C/180°C fan-forced. Oil six-hole (¾-cup/180ml) texas muffin pan.
3 Cut two 13cm rounds from opposite corners of each pastry sheet; cut two 9cm rounds from remaining corners of each sheet. Place the six large rounds in muffin pan holes to cover bases and sides; trim any excess pastry. Lightly prick bases with fork; refrigerate 30 minutes. Cover the six small rounds with a damp cloth.
4 Cover pastry-lined pan holes with baking paper; fill holes with uncooked rice or dried beans. Bake, uncovered, 10 minutes; remove paper and rice. Cool.
5 Spoon mince filling into holes; brush edges with a little egg. Top pies with small pastry rounds; gently press around edges to seal.
6 Brush pies with remaining egg; bake, uncovered, about 15 minutes or until browned lightly. Stand in pan 5 minutes before serving with mashed potatoes, if you like.

preparation time *15 minutes (plus refrigeration time)*
cooking time *45 minutes* makes *6*
nutritional count per serving *28.6g total fat (13.2g saturated fat); 1977kJ (473 cal); 35.5g carbohydrate; 17.5g protein; 2.9g fibre*

rissoles with cabbage mash

Rissoles can be prepared a day ahead and kept, covered, in the refrigerator.

2 rindless bacon rashers (130g), chopped finely
1 small brown onion (80g), chopped finely
1 clove garlic, crushed
1 fresh small red thai chilli, chopped finely
1 tablespoon worcestershire sauce
1 cup (70g) stale breadcrumbs
1 egg
¼ cup coarsely chopped fresh flat-leaf parsley
500g beef mince
2 tablespoons barbecue sauce
1 tablespoon vegetable oil
1 tablespoon dijon mustard
2 cups (500ml) beef stock
1 tablespoon cornflour
2 tablespoons water
cabbage mash
1kg potatoes, quartered
¼ cup (60ml) cream
30g butter, chopped
200g finely shredded savoy cabbage
1 small white onion (80g), chopped finely

1 Cook potato for cabbage mash.
2 Meanwhile, cook bacon, onion, garlic and chilli in medium frying pan, stirring until onion softens. Remove from heat.
3 Combine worcestershire sauce, breadcrumbs, egg, parsley, mince and half of the barbecue sauce with bacon mixture in large bowl; shape mixture into eight rissoles.
4 Heat oil in same pan; cook rissoles, in batches, until browned both sides and cooked through. Cover to keep warm.
5 Place mustard, stock and remaining barbecue sauce in same pan; bring to the boil. Stir in blended cornflour and water; cook, stirring, until gravy boils and thickens slightly.
6 Finish cabbage mash. Top rissoles with gravy; serve with cabbage mash.

cabbage mash Boil, steam or microwave potato until tender; drain. Mash potato with cream and butter until smooth; stir in cabbage and onion.

preparation time *25 minutes*
cooking time *20 minutes* serves *4*
nutritional count per serving *32.9g total fat (14.8g saturated fat); 2939kJ (703 cal); 53.5g carbohydrate; 44.7g protein; 7.1g fibre*

burgers with mustard mayonnaise

1 Combine mince, stuffing mix, sauce and parsley in medium bowl. Shape mixture into four patties.
2 Cook patties on heated oiled barbecue, uncovered, until browned and cooked through.
3 Meanwhile, cook onion on heated oiled barbecue plate until soft and browned.
4 Split buns in half. Place each half, cut-side down, onto barbecue; cook until lightly toasted.
5 Sandwich lettuce, tomato, patties, combined mustard and mayonnaise and onion between bun halves.

preparation time *20 minutes*
cooking time *15 minutes* serves *4*
nutritional count per serving *26.4g total fat (6.8g saturated fat); 2378kJ (569 cal); 98.9g carbohydrate; 31.5g protein; 4.9g fibre*

burgers with mustard mayonnaise

500g beef mince
½ cup (40g) packaged seasoned stuffing mix
¼ cup (70ml) tomato sauce
¼ cup coarsely chopped fresh flat-leaf parsley
2 large white onions (400g), thinly sliced
4 hamburger buns
8 green oak leaf lettuce leaves
1 large tomato (220g), thinly sliced
1 tablespoon wholegrain mustard
½ cup (150g) mayonnaise

rissole, bacon and tomato casserole

600g beef mince
1 small brown onion (80g), chopped finely
1 egg
½ cup (100g) white long-grain rice
¼ cup (15g) stale breadcrumbs
2 teaspoons worcestershire sauce
4 rindless bacon rashers (260g), chopped finely
400g can diced tomatoes
½ cup (125ml) beef stock
2 tablespoons tomato paste
½ cup coarsely chopped fresh basil

1 Preheat oven to 200°C/180°C fan-forced.
2 Combine mince, onion, egg, rice, breadcrumbs and sauce in large bowl. Shape mixture into 12 rissoles; place into deep 2-litre (8-cup) ovenproof dish.
3 Sprinkle bacon over rissoles; pour over combined tomatoes, stock and paste.
4 Bake casserole, covered, 1 hour or until rissoles are cooked through and rice is tender. Stir in basil before serving.

preparation time *15 minutes*
cooking time *1 hour* serves *4*
nutritional count per serving *24.8g total fat (10g saturated fat); 2190kJ (524 cal); 28.7g carbohydrate; 45.3g protein; 2.4g fibre*

rissole, bacon and tomato casserole

spinach and chicken lasagne

2 teaspoons olive oil

1 medium brown onion (150g), coarsely chopped

1 clove garlic, crushed

1kg chicken mince

2 x 415g cans diced tomatoes

2 tablespoons tomato paste

1 teaspoon dried oregano

1 teaspoon dried basil

500g spinach

60g butter

¼ cup (35g) plain flour

2 cups (500ml) milk

1 cup (120g) coarsely grated cheddar cheese

175g instant lasagne sheets

1 Heat oil in large pan; cook onion and garlic, stirring, until onion is soft. Add mince; cook, stirring, until mince is changed in colour. Stir in undrained tomatoes, paste, oregano and basil; simmer, uncovered, stirring occasionally, about 30 minutes or until most of the liquid is absorbed.

2 Meanwhile, trim spinach; discard stems. Boil, steam or microwave spinach until just wilted; drain. Squeeze excess liquid from spinach; chop coarsely.

3 Melt butter in small saucepan. Add flour; cook, stirring, until mixture thickens and bubbles. Gradually stir in milk; stir until mixture boils and thickens. Remove from heat; stir in cheese and spinach.

4 Preheat oven to 180°C/160°C fan-forced.

5 Place a third of the lasagne sheets over base of oiled shallow 2-litre (8-cup) ovenproof dish. Cover with half the mince mixture, top with a third of the spinach mixture. Repeat with another third of the lasagne sheets, remaining mince mixture and a third of spinach mixture. Top with remaining lasagne sheets and spinach mixture. (Can be made ahead to this stage. Cover; refrigerate overnight or freeze.)

6 Cover lasagne with foil; bake 40 minutes. Remove foil; bake about 30 minutes or until browned lightly.

preparation time *40 minutes*

cooking time *2 hours* serves *4*

nutritional count per serving *51.7g total fat (24.5g saturated fat); 4109kJ (983 cal); 53.9g carbohydrate; 71.7g protein; 8.7g fibre*

oven-baked risotto with italian sausages

500g spicy italian-style sausages
1 litre (4 cups) chicken stock
1 tablespoon olive oil
40g butter
2 large brown onions (400g), chopped coarsely
1 clove garlic, crushed
2 cups (400g) arborio rice
¾ cup (180ml) dry white wine
1 cup (150g) drained semi-dried tomatoes
¼ cup loosely packed fresh basil leaves
¼ cup (20g) coarsely grated parmesan cheese

1 Preheat oven to 180°C/160°C fan-forced.
2 Heat flameproof dish on stove top; cook sausages until browned all over and cooked through. Remove from dish; slice thickly.
3 Meanwhile, add stock to medium saucepan; bring to the boil.
4 Heat oil and butter in same flameproof dish; cook onion and garlic, stirring, until soft. Add rice; stir to coat in onion mixture. Add wine, bring to the boil then simmer, uncovered, 1 minute. Add stock, sausages and tomatoes; cover, transfer dish to oven. Bake about 25 minutes or until liquid is absorbed and rice is tender. Stir once during baking.
5 Stir in the basil and cheese.

preparation time *15 minutes*
cooking time *40 minutes* serves *6*
nutritional count per serving *36.8g total fat (14.4g saturated fat); 3114kJ (745 cal); 68.6g carbohydrate; 27.3g protein; 5.5g fibre*

rissoles with grilled onions

4 Meanwhile, heat oil on barbecue flat plate; cook onions, stirring, until browned lightly. Add sugar and vinegar; cook, stirring, about 5 minutes or until onions caramelise.

5 Serve rissoles with grilled onions. Accompany with a leafy green salad, or mashed potato and gravy.

preparation time *15 minutes*
cooking time *15 minutes* serves *4*
nutritional count per serving *19.6g total fat (6.4g saturated fat); 1923kJ (460 cal); 31.7g carbohydrate; 37.8g protein; 2.7g fibre*

rissoles with grilled onions

2 rindless bacon rashers (130g), chopped finely
1 small brown onion (80g), chopped finely
500g beef mince
1 cup (70g) stale breadcrumbs
1 egg
2 tablespoons barbecue sauce
1 tablespoon worcestershire sauce
1 tablespoon olive oil
3 medium brown onions (450g), sliced thinly
2 tablespoons brown sugar
1 tablespoon brown malt vinegar

1 Cook bacon and onion in oiled medium frying pan, stirring, until onion softens. Cool.
2 Combine mince, breadcrumbs, egg, sauces and bacon mixture in large bowl; shape into 12 rissoles.
3 Cook rissoles on heated oiled barbecue grill plate until cooked through.

grilled pork sausages with fruit relish

1 tablespoon olive oil
1 small red onion (100g), chopped finely
1 clove garlic, crushed
2 medium pears (460g), chopped finely
¼ cup (40g) finely chopped dried apricots
¼ cup (40g) sultanas, chopped finely
2 tablespoons cider vinegar
2 tablespoons brown sugar
½ teaspoon ground allspice
12 thick pork sausages (1.5kg)

1 Heat oil in medium saucepan; cook onion and garlic, stirring, until onions soften. Add fruit, vinegar, sugar and spice; cook, uncovered, stirring occasionally, about 10 minutes or until mixture is thick and pulpy.
2 Meanwhile, cook sausages on heated oiled grill plate (or grill or barbecue) until cooked through.
3 Serve sausages with fruit relish.

preparation time *10 minutes*
cooking time *20 minutes* serves *6*
nutritional count per serving *58.7g total fat (22.9g saturated fat); 3252kJ (778 cal); 29.9g carbohydrate; 31g protein; 6.2g fibre*

grilled pork sausages with fruit relish

pork cabbage rolls

Preserved lemon is a North African speciality: it imparts a rich salty-sour acidic flavour to food. Lemon is preserved in a mixture of salt and lemon juice; remove and discard pulp, squeeze juice from rind, rinse rind well then slice thinly.

18 large cabbage leaves
½ cup (100g) white long-grain rice
250g pork mince
1 medium brown onion (150g), chopped finely
¼ cup finely chopped fresh dill
1 clove garlic, crushed
1 tablespoon tomato paste
2 teaspoons ground cumin
1 teaspoon ground coriander
1 teaspoon ground allspice
4 cloves garlic, quartered
2 medium tomatoes (300g), chopped coarsely
2 x 400g cans crushed tomatoes
¼ cup (60ml) lemon juice

1 Discard thick stems from 15 cabbage leaves; reserve remaining leaves. Boil, steam or microwave trimmed leaves until just pliable; drain. Rinse under cold water; drain. Pat dry with absorbent paper.

2 Combine rice, mince, onion, dill, crushed garlic, paste and spices in medium bowl.

3 Place one trimmed leaf, vein-side up, on board; cut leaf in half lengthways. Place 1 rounded teaspoon of the mince mixture at stem end of each half; roll each half firmly to enclose filling. Repeat with remaining trimmed leaves.

4 Place reserved leaves in base of large saucepan. Place only enough rolls, seam-side down, in single layer, to completely cover leaves in base of saucepan. Top with quartered garlic, chopped fresh tomato then remaining rolls.

5 Pour undrained tomatoes and juice over cabbage rolls; bring to the boil. Reduce heat; simmer, covered, 1 hour. Uncover; simmer about 30 minutes or until cabbage rolls are cooked through.

6 Serve rolls with thick greek-style yogurt flavoured with a little finely chopped preserved lemon, or finely grated lemon rind, if you like.

preparation time *1 hour*
cooking time *1 hour 40 minutes* serves *6*
nutritional count per serving *3.6g total fat (1.1g saturated fat); 803kJ (192 cal); 24.7g carbohydrates; 14.3g protein; 9.7g fibre*

meatballs in spicy coconut milk

Fried shallots are served as a condiment at Asian mealtimes or sprinkled over just-cooked food to provide an extra crunchy finish to a salad, stir-fry or curry. They can be purchased at all Asian grocery stores; once opened, they will keep for months if stored in a tightly sealed glass jar. Make your own by frying thinly sliced peeled shallots or baby onions until golden brown and crisp.

800g beef mince
2 eggs
2 teaspoons cornflour
2 cloves garlic, crushed
1 tablespoon finely chopped fresh coriander
1 fresh long red chilli, chopped finely
2 shallots (50g), chopped coarsely
3 cloves garlic, quartered
1 teaspoon chilli flakes
7 fresh long red chillies, chopped coarsely
2 tablespoons peanut oil
2cm piece fresh galangal (10g), sliced thinly
3 large tomatoes (660g), seeded,
    chopped coarsely
400ml can coconut milk
1 tablespoon kecap asin
1 large tomato (220g), seeded, diced
½ cup (40g) fried shallots
1 fresh small red chilli, sliced thinly

1 Combine mince, eggs, cornflour, crushed garlic, coriander and finely chopped chilli in medium bowl; roll level tablespoons of mixture into balls. Place meatballs, in single layer, in large baking-paper-lined bamboo steamer. Steam, covered, over wok of simmering water 10 minutes.

2 Meanwhile, blend or process shallots, quartered garlic, chilli flakes, coarsely chopped chilli and half the oil until mixture forms a paste.

3 Heat remaining oil in wok; cook shallot paste and galangal, stirring, about 1 minute or until fragrant. Add chopped tomato; cook, stirring, 1 minute. Add coconut milk, kecap asin and meatballs; simmer, uncovered, stirring occasionally, about 5 minutes or until meatballs are cooked through and sauce thickens slightly.

4 Serve curry topped with diced tomato, fried shallots and thinly sliced chilli.

preparation time *25 minutes*
cooking time *20 minutes* serves *4*
nutritional count per serving *47.1g total fat (26.5g saturated fat); 2721kJ (651 cal); 8.3g carbohydrate; 47.7g protein; 3.9g fibre*

chilli rice noodles with buk choy

1 Place noodles in medium heatproof bowl; cover with boiling water, separate with fork, drain.
2 Heat oil in wok; stir-fry mince until browned. Add garlic and chilli; stir-fry until fragrant. Add noodles, buk choy, tamari, sauce and kecap manis; stir-fry until buk choy just wilts.
3 Remove from heat; stir in onion, basil and sprouts.
preparation time *20 minutes*
cooking time *15 minutes* serves *4*
nutritional count per serving *14.4g total fat (4.7g saturated fat); 1877kJ (449 cal); 44.5g carbohydrate; 34.3g protein; 5.3g fibre*

nepalese pork mince curry

This dry, fragrant Nepalese curry, made with pork mince and usually served with steamed rice and lime wedges, is one of this small Himalayan country's most popular meat dishes.

2 tablespoons peanut oil
2 tablespoons yellow mustard seeds
2 teaspoons ground cumin
1 teaspoon ground turmeric
2 teaspoons garam masala
3 cloves garlic, crushed
4cm piece fresh ginger (20g), grated
2 medium brown onions (300g), chopped finely
800g pork mince
½ cup (125ml) water
¼ cup coarsely chopped fresh coriander

chilli rice noodles with buk choy

Fresh rice noodles are found in the refrigerated sections of supermarkets and Asian grocery stores. Because they're fresh and not dried, they do not need to be reconstituted by cooking, nor do they require a lengthy soaking time.

400g fresh thin rice noodles
1 tablespoon peanut oil
500g lamb mince
3 cloves garlic, crushed
2 fresh small red thai chillies, chopped finely
400g buk choy, sliced thinly
2 tablespoons tamari
1 tablespoon fish sauce
2 tablespoons kecap manis
4 green onions, sliced thinly
1 cup firmly packed thai basil leaves
3 cups (240g) bean sprouts

1 Heat oil in large frying pan; cook seeds, stirring, about 2 minutes or until seeds pop. Add cumin, turmeric and garam masala; cook, stirring, 2 minutes.
2 Add garlic, ginger and onion to pan; cook, stirring, until onion softens. Add mince; cook, stirring, until cooked through. Add the water; simmer, uncovered, 15 minutes. Remove from heat, stir in coriander.
preparation time *15 minutes*
cooking time *20 minutes* serves *4*
nutritional count per serving *23.4g total fat (6.9g saturated fat); 1655kJ (396 cal); 4g carbohydrate; 41.4g protein; 2.6g fibre*

nepalese pork mince curry

cottage pie

You can make the cottage pie up to two days in advance; keep, covered, in the refrigerator. Reheat, covered, in a moderately slow oven for about 40 minutes. The pie can also be frozen for up to three months; thaw overnight in the refrigerator before reheating as above.

1 tablespoon olive oil
2 cloves garlic, crushed
1 large brown onion (200g), chopped finely
2 medium carrots (240g), chopped finely
1kg beef mince
1 tablespoon worcestershire sauce
2 tablespoons tomato paste
2 x 425g cans crushed tomatoes
1 teaspoon dried mixed herbs
200g button mushrooms, quartered
1 cup (120g) frozen peas
1kg sebago potatoes, chopped coarsely
¾ cup (180ml) hot milk
40g butter, softened
½ cup (50g) coarsely grated pizza cheese

1 Heat oil in large saucepan; cook garlic, onion and carrot, stirring, until onion softens. Add mince; cook, stirring, about 10 minutes or until changed in colour.
2 Add sauce, paste, undrained tomatoes and herbs; bring to the boil. Reduce heat; simmer, uncovered, about 30 minutes or until mixture thickens slightly. Stir in mushrooms and peas.
3 Meanwhile, preheat oven to 180°C/160°C fan-forced.
4 Boil, steam or microwave potato until tender; drain. Mash potato in large bowl with milk and butter.
5 Pour mince mixture into deep 3-litre (12-cup) ovenproof dish; top with mashed potato mixture, sprinkle with cheese. Bake, uncovered, in oven about 45 minutes or until pie is heated through and top is browned lightly.

preparation time *20 minutes*
cooking time *1 hour 35 minutes* serves *8*
nutritional count per serving *16.5g total fat (7.6g saturated fat); 1659kJ (397 cal); 23.9g carbohydrate; 35.2g protein; 6g fibre*

potato and beef pasties

You can also use pink-eye or sebago potatoes for this recipe.

500g coliban potatoes, chopped coarsely
1 tablespoon olive oil
1 small brown onion (80g), chopped finely
2 cloves garlic, crushed
1 medium carrot (120g), chopped finely
1 stalk celery (150g), trimmed, chopped finely
350g beef mince
⅓ cup (80ml) dry red wine
1 cup (250ml) beef stock
¼ cup (70g) tomato paste
½ cup (60g) frozen peas
8 sheets ready-rolled puff pastry, thawed
1 egg, beaten lightly

1 Boil, steam or microwave potato until tender; drain. Mash in medium bowl.
2 Meanwhile, heat oil in medium saucepan; cook onion and garlic, stirring, until onion softens. Add carrot and celery; cook, stirring, until vegetables are tender. Add mince; cook, stirring, until changed in colour.
3 Stir in wine, stock, paste and peas; cook, uncovered, about 5 minutes or until mixture thickens slightly. Stir potato into beef mixture; cool 10 minutes.
4 Preheat oven to 180°C/160°C fan-forced. Lightly oil two oven trays.
5 Cut two 14cm-rounds from one pastry sheet; place rounds on oven tray. Place about one-sixteenth of the filling in centre of each round. Brush edge of pastry with egg; fold over to enclose filling, pressing around edge with fork to seal. Repeat process with remaining pastry sheets, one at a time, and remaining filling.
6 Bake pasties, uncovered, about 30 minutes or until browned lightly.

preparation time *30 minutes*
cooking time *45 minutes* makes *16*
nutritional count per pastie *22g total fat (11.1g saturated fat); 1626kJ (389 cal); 34.9g carbohydrate; 10.9g protein; 2.3g fibre*

stews

beef and onion casserole

1kg beef chuck steak, cut into 2cm dice

⅓ cup (50g) plain flour

2 tablespoons olive oil

2 small brown onions (160g), chopped coarsely

2 cloves garlic, crushed

150g button mushrooms, quartered

1 cup (250ml) dry red wine

400g can crushed tomatoes

2 cups (500ml) beef stock

2 tablespoons tomato paste

1 Coat beef in flour, shake away excess. Heat half the oil in large saucepan; cook beef, in batches, until browned all over. Heat remaining oil in same pan; cook onion, garlic and mushrooms, stirring, until onion softens.

2 Return beef to pan with wine, undrained tomatoes, stock and paste; bring to the boil. Reduce heat; simmer, covered, 40 minutes. Uncover; simmer about 40 minutes or until meat is tender and sauce thickens slightly, stirring occasionally.

preparation time *20 minutes*

cooking time *1 hour 30 minutes* serves *4*

nutritional count per serving *21.2g total fat (6.2g saturated fat); 2245kJ (537 cal); 17.4g carbohydrate; 56.8g protein; 4g fibre*

tuscan beef stew

1 tablespoon olive oil
400g spring onions, trimmed
1kg chuck steak, cut into 3cm cubes
30g butter
2 tablespoons plain flour
2 cups (500ml) dry red wine
1 cup (250ml) beef stock
1 cup (250ml) water
2 cloves garlic, crushed
6 sprigs thyme
2 bay leaves
1 stalk celery (150g), trimmed, chopped coarsely
400g baby carrots, trimmed, halved
2 cups (240g) frozen peas
⅓ cup coarsely chopped fresh flat-leaf parsley

1 Heat oil in large heavy-based saucepan; cook onions, stirring occasionally, about 10 minutes or until browned lightly, remove from pan. Cook steak, in batches, over high heat in same pan, until browned all over.

2 Melt butter in same saucepan, add flour; cook, stirring, until mixture bubbles and thickens. Gradually stir in wine, stock and the water; stir until mixture boils and thickens. Return steak to pan with garlic, thyme and bay leaves. Bring to the boil then reduce heat; simmer, covered, 1½ hours.

3 Add onion to pan with celery and carrot; simmer, covered, 30 minutes. Add peas; simmer, uncovered, until peas are just tender. Stir in parsley just before serving. Serve with penne pasta, if you like.

preparation time *15 minutes*
cooking time *2 hours 40 minutes* serves *4*
nutritional count per serving *22.6g total fat (9.5g saturated fat); 2504kJ (599 cal); 16.4g carbohydrate; 57.4g protein; 9g fibre*

beef and red wine casserole

You could also use round or chuck steak.

2 cups (500ml) water
1kg skirt steak, trimmed, cut into 3cm cubes
2 medium brown onions (300g), sliced thickly
2 tablespoons olive oil
6 cloves garlic, crushed
2 cups (500ml) beef stock
2 cups (500ml) dry red wine
½ cup (140g) tomato paste
1 tablespoon finely chopped fresh rosemary
1 tablespoon finely chopped fresh flat-leaf parsley
500g fresh fettuccine pasta

1 Combine the water, steak, onion, oil, garlic, stock, wine and paste in deep 3-litre (12-cup) microwave-safe dish; cook, covered, on HIGH (100%) for 50 minutes, stirring every 15 minutes to ensure steak remains covered in cooking liquid. Uncover; cook on HIGH (100%) about 10 minutes or until steak is tender. Stir in herbs.
2 During final 10 minutes of casserole cooking time, cook pasta in large saucepan of boiling water until tender; drain.
3 Divide pasta among dishes; top with casserole.
preparation time *20 minutes*
cooking time *1 hour* serves *4*
nutritional count per serving *16.3g total fat (4.1g saturated fat); 3010kJ (720 cal); 6.4g carbohydrate; 8.4g protein; 51.5g fibre*

chicken and vegetable pasties

2 teaspoons vegetable oil

2 cloves garlic, crushed

1 medium brown onion (150g), chopped finely

1½ cups (240g) coarsely chopped leftover cooked chicken

2 cups (240g) frozen pea, corn and carrot mixture

2 teaspoons dijon mustard

½ cup (120g) sour cream

¼ cup (30g) coarsely grated cheddar cheese

4 sheets ready-rolled puff pastry

1 egg, beaten lightly

1 Preheat oven to 220°C/200°C fan-forced. Lightly oil oven tray.

2 Heat oil in large frying pan; cook garlic and onion, stirring, until onion softens. Add chicken, frozen vegetables, mustard, sour cream and cheese; stir until heated through.

3 Cut one 22cm round from each pastry sheet. Place a quarter of the filling in centre of each round. Brush edge of pastry with egg; fold over to enclose filling, pinching edge together to seal.

4 Place pasties on tray; brush with remaining egg. Bake in oven about 30 minutes or until browned lightly.

preparation time *15 minutes*

cooking time *30 minutes* makes *4*

nutritional count per pastie *62.5g total fat (32.3g saturated fat); 4063kJ (972 cal); 69.1g carbohydrate; 31.4g protein; 5.9g fibre*

massaman curry

1kg skirt steak, cut into 3cm pieces
2 cups (500ml) beef stock
5 cardamom pods, bruised
¼ teaspoon ground clove
2 star anise
1 tablespoon grated palm sugar
2 tablespoons fish sauce
2 tablespoons tamarind concentrate
2 x 400ml cans coconut milk
2 tablespoons massaman curry paste
8 baby brown onions (200g), halved
1 medium kumara (400g), chopped coarsely
¼ cup (35g) coarsely chopped roasted
    unsalted peanuts
2 green onions, sliced thinly

1 Place beef, 1½ cups of the stock, cardamom, clove, star anise, sugar, sauce, 1 tablespoon of the tamarind and half the coconut milk in large saucepan; simmer, uncovered, about 1½ hours or until beef is almost tender.
2 Strain beef over large bowl; reserve 1 cup of the braising liquid, discard solids. Cover beef to keep warm.
3 Cook curry paste in same pan, stirring until fragrant. Add remaining coconut milk, tamarind and stock; bring to the boil. Cook, stirring, about 1 minute or until mixture is smooth. Return beef to pan with brown onion, kumara and reserved braising liquid; simmer, uncovered, about 30 minutes or until beef and vegetables are tender.
4 Remove from heat; stir in nuts and green onion.
preparation time *20 minutes*
cooking time *2 hours 10 minutes* serves *4*
nutritional count per serving *52.7g total fat (39.5g saturated fat); 3645kJ (872 cal); 29.2g carbohydrate; 67.4g protein; 7.2g fibre*

Many curry pastes are available in various strengths from supermarkets. Use whichever one suits your heat-level tolerance best.

beef carbonade pies

Stout is a strong, dark beer that originated in Great Britain in the late 1700s. More redolent of hops than other beers, it is made with roasted barley, giving it its characteristic dark colour and bitter-sweet, almost coffee-like flavour.

2kg beef round steak, diced into 3cm pieces
½ cup (75g) plain flour
40g butter, melted
¼ cup (60ml) vegetable oil
4 medium brown onions (600g), sliced thickly
2 large carrots (360g), chopped coarsely
2 cloves garlic, crushed
2¾ cups (680ml) stout
2 tablespoons brown sugar
¼ cup (60ml) cider vinegar
3 sprigs fresh thyme
1 bay leaf
2 sheets ready-rolled puff pastry
1 tablespoon milk
1 egg, beaten lightly

1 Coat beef in flour; shake off excess. Heat butter and 2 tablespoons of the oil in large deep saucepan; cook beef, in batches, until browned all over.
2 Heat remaining oil in same pan; cook onion, carrot and garlic, stirring, until onion softens. Return beef to pan with stout, sugar, vinegar, thyme and bay leaf; bring to the boil. Reduce heat; simmer, covered, 1½ hours.
3 Uncover; simmer, stirring occasionally, about 1 hour or until beef is tender and sauce thickens. Discard herbs.
4 Preheat oven to 220°C/200°C fan-forced.
5 Divide beef mixture among eight 1¼-cup (310ml) ovenproof dishes. Cut each pastry sheet into four squares; top each dish with one pastry square. Brush pastry with combined milk and egg; place dishes on oven tray. Bake, uncovered, about 15 minutes or until pastry is puffed and browned lightly.

preparation time *25 minutes*
cooking time *3 hours 20 minutes* serves *8*
nutritional count per serving *33.9g total fat (14.4g saturated fat); 2930 kJ (701 cal); 32.4g carbohydrates; 58.2g protein; 3.1g fibre*

moussaka

2 large eggplants (1kg), sliced thinly
1 tablespoon coarse cooking salt
¼ cup (60ml) olive oil
1 large brown onion (200g), chopped finely
2 cloves garlic, crushed
1kg lamb mince
425g can crushed tomatoes
½ cup (125ml) dry white wine
1 teaspoon ground cinnamon
¼ cup (20g) finely grated parmesan cheese
white sauce
80g butter
⅓ cup (50g) plain flour
2 cups (500ml) milk

1 Place eggplant in colander, sprinkle all over with salt; stand 30 minutes. Rinse under cold water; drain. Pat dry with absorbent paper.
2 Heat oil in large frying pan; cook eggplant, in batches, until browned both sides; drain on absorbent paper.
3 Cook onion and garlic in same pan, stirring, until onion softens. Add mince; cook, stirring, until mince changes colour. Stir in undrained tomatoes, wine and cinnamon; bring to the boil then simmer, uncovered, about 30 minutes or until liquid has evaporated.
4 Meanwhile, preheat oven to 180°C/160°C fan-forced. Oil 2-litre (8-cup) shallow ovenproof dish.
5 Make white sauce.
6 Place a third of the eggplant, overlapping slices slightly, in prepared dish; spread half the meat sauce over eggplant. Repeat layering with another third of the eggplant, remaining meat sauce and remaining eggplant. Spread white sauce over top layer of eggplant; sprinkle with cheese. Cook, uncovered, in oven, about 40 minutes or until top browns lightly. Cover moussaka; stand 10 minutes before serving.
white sauce Melt butter in medium saucepan. Add flour; cook, stirring, until mixture thickens and bubbles. Gradually add milk; stir until mixture boils and thickens.
preparation time *40 minutes (plus standing time)*
cooking time *1 hour 30 minutes* serves *6*
nutritional count per serving *36.6g total fat (16.5g saturated fat); 2420kJ (579 cal); 18g carbohydrate; 41.8g protein; 5.3g fibre*

beef vindaloo curry

The curry is best made a day ahead to allow its flavour to develop fully. Round steak and skirt steak are also suitable for this recipe.

2 teaspoons cumin seeds
2 teaspoons garam masala
4 cardamom pods, bruised
1 tablespoon grated fresh ginger
6 cloves garlic, crushed
8 fresh small red thai chillies, chopped finely
2 tablespoons white vinegar
1 tablespoon tamarind concentrate
1.5kg chuck steak, cut into 3cm cubes
2 tablespoons ghee
2 large brown onions (400g), chopped finely
1 cinnamon stick
6 cloves
2 teaspoons plain flour
3 cups (750ml) beef stock

1 Dry-fry cumin, garam masala and cardamom in heated large frying pan, stirring, until fragrant. Combine roasted spices with ginger, garlic, chilli, vinegar and tamarind in large bowl; add steak, toss to coat steak in marinade. Cover; refrigerate 1 hour or overnight.

2 Melt ghee in large frying pan; cook onion, cinnamon and cloves, stirring, until onion is browned lightly. Add steak mixture; cook, stirring, until steak is browned all over. Stir in flour; cook, stirring, 2 minutes. Gradually add stock; bring to the boil, stirring. Reduce heat; simmer, uncovered, 1 hour. Vindaloo is great served with dhal, raita and a bowl of crisp pappadums.

preparation time *40 minutes (plus refrigeration time)*
cooking time *3 hours 20 minutes* serves *4*
nutrition count per serving *26.2g total fat
(13.1g saturated fat); 2500kJ (598 cal);
8.9g carbohydrate; 8.1g protein; 2.5g fibre*

lamb and rosemary pies with peas

2 tablespoons olive oil

400g diced lamb

4 baby onions (100g), quartered

1 tablespoon plain flour

¼ cup (60ml) dry red wine

¾ cup (180ml) beef stock

1 tablespoon tomato paste

1 tablespoon fresh rosemary leaves

2 sheets ready-rolled puff pastry

1 egg, beaten lightly

4 fresh rosemary sprigs

20g butter

2½ cups (300g) frozen peas

1 tablespoon lemon juice

½ cup (125ml) water

1 Heat half the oil in large saucepan; cook lamb, in batches, uncovered, until browned all over. Heat remaining oil in same pan; cook onion, stirring, until soft. Add flour; cook, stirring, until mixture bubbles and thickens. Gradually add wine, stock, paste and rosemary leaves; stir until mixture boils and thickens. Stir in lamb; cool 10 minutes.

2 Preheat oven to 200°C/180°C fan-forced. Oil four holes of six-hole ¾-cup (180ml) texas muffin pan.

3 Cut two 13cm rounds from opposite corners of each pastry sheet; cut two 9cm rounds from remaining corners of each sheet. Place larger rounds in prepared pan holes to cover bases and sides; trim any excess pastry, prick bases with fork.

4 Spoon lamb mixture into pastry cases; brush around edges with a little egg. Top pies with smaller rounds; gently press around edges to seal. Brush pies with remaining egg; press one rosemary sprig into top of each pie.

5 Bake pies, uncovered, about 15 minutes or until browned lightly. Stand in pan 5 minutes before serving.

6 Meanwhile, heat butter in medium saucepan, add peas, juice and the water; cook, uncovered, stirring occasionally, about 5 minutes or until peas are just tender. Serve with mashed potatoes, if you like.

preparation time *20 minutes*

cooking time *25 minutes* serves *4*

nutritional count per serving *42.7g total fat (18.6g saturated fat); 2868kJ (686 cal); 40.4g carbohydrate; 33.1g protein; 6.1g fibre*

mexican beans with sausages

1 cup (200g) dried kidney beans
800g beef sausages, chopped coarsely
1 tablespoon olive oil
1 large brown onion (200g), chopped coarsely
3 cloves garlic, crushed
1 large red capsicum (350g), chopped coarsely
½ teaspoon ground cumin
2 teaspoons sweet smoked paprika
1 teaspoon dried chilli flakes
2 x 400g cans crushed tomatoes
2 tablespoons coarsely chopped fresh oregano

1 Place beans in medium bowl, cover with cold water; stand overnight, drain. Rinse under cold water; drain. Place beans in medium saucepan of boiling water; return to the boil. Reduce heat; simmer, uncovered, about 30 minutes or until beans are almost tender. Drain.

2 Cook sausages, in batches, in oiled large deep saucepan until browned; drain on absorbent paper.

3 Heat oil in same pan; cook onion, garlic and capsicum, stirring, until onion softens. Add cumin, paprika and chilli; cook, stirring, about 2 minutes or until fragrant. Add beans and undrained tomatoes; bring to the boil. Reduce heat; simmer, covered, about 1 hour or until beans are tender.

4 Return sausages to pan; simmer, covered, about 10 minutes or until sausages are cooked through. Remove from heat; stir in oregano. Serve with tortillas, if you like.

preparation time *20 minutes (plus standing time)* cooking time *2 hours 15 minutes* serves *4* nutritional count per serving *56.9g total fat (25.2g saturated fat); 3323 kJ (795 cal); 33.5g carbohydrates; 38.1g protein; 20.2g fibre*

anchovy and chilli lamb neck chops with creamy polenta

Serve the chops with mashed potato instead of the polenta, if you prefer.

4 anchovy fillets, drained, chopped finely
2 fresh small red thai chillies, chopped finely
4 cloves garlic, crushed
½ cup (125ml) dry red wine
8 lamb neck chops (1.4kg), trimmed
2 tablespoons olive oil
1 medium brown onion (150g), chopped coarsely
1 tablespoon plain flour
400g can crushed tomatoes
2 cups (500ml) beef stock
2 cups (500ml) milk
2 cups (500ml) water
1 cup (170g) polenta
½ cup (40g) finely grated parmesan cheese
½ cup (125ml) cream
½ cup coarsely chopped fresh flat-leaf parsley

1 Combine anchovy, chilli, garlic and wine in medium bowl, add lamb; turn lamb to coat in marinade. Cover; refrigerate 3 hours or overnight.
2 Preheat oven to 160°C/140°C fan-forced.
3 Heat half the oil in deep medium baking dish; cook undrained lamb, in batches, until browned all over. Heat remaining oil in same dish; cook onion, stirring, until softened. Add flour; cook, stirring, about 5 minutes or until mixture browns lightly.
4 Return lamb to dish with undrained tomatoes and stock, cover; cook in oven 1½ hours.
5 Uncover, skim fat from surface; cook, turning lamb occasionally, about 30 minutes or until lamb is tender.
6 Meanwhile, combine milk and the water in large saucepan; bring to the boil. Gradually add polenta to liquid, stirring constantly. Reduce heat; simmer, stirring, about 5 minutes or until polenta thickens. Stir in cheese, cream and parsley.
7 Divide polenta among serving plates, top with lamb; sprinkle with extra coarsely chopped fresh flat-leaf parsley to serve, if you like.

preparation time *20 minutes (plus refrigeration time)* cooking time *2 hours 25 minutes* serves *4* nutritional count per serving *43.1g total fat (19.4g saturated fat); 3791kJ (907 cal); 45g carbohydrate; 79.9g protein; 3.9g fibre*

green chilli stew

Round steak, skirt steak and gravy beef are also suitable for this recipe. Tortilla crisps can be prepared up to two days ahead and kept in an airtight container at room temperature.

2 tablespoons olive oil
1kg chuck steak, cut into 3cm cubes
1 large brown onion (200g), sliced thinly
2 cloves garlic, sliced thinly
2 teaspoons ground cumin
2 long green chillies, sliced thinly
2 cups (500ml) beef stock
1 tablespoon tomato paste
3 large egg tomatoes (270g), chopped coarsely
500g baby new potatoes, halved
4 small flour tortillas
¼ cup coarsely chopped fresh coriander

1 Heat half the oil in large flameproof baking dish; cook steak, in batches, stirring, until browned all over.
2 Preheat oven to 180°C/160°C fan-forced.
3 Heat remaining oil in same dish; cook onion, garlic, cumin and chilli, stirring, until onion softens. Add stock and paste; bring to the boil, stirring. Return steak to dish, cover; cook, in oven, 45 minutes.
4 Add tomato and potato; cook, covered, 35 minutes. Uncover; cook 20 minutes.
5 Meanwhile, cut each tortilla into six wedges. Place, in single layer, on oven trays; toast, uncovered, in oven about 8 minutes or until crisp.
6 Stir coriander into stew just before serving with tortilla crisps and, if you like, grilled cobs of corn.
preparation time *15 minutes*
cooking time *1 hour 40 minutes* serves *4*
nutritional count per serving *23.4g total fat (6.6g saturated fat); 2604kJ (623 cal); 40.1g carbohydrate; 59.8g protein; 5.6g fibre*

hearty beef stew with red wine and mushrooms

The rich combination of stock and wine, plus the long, slow cooking time, gives this stew its robust intensity. Rump steak or round steak are also suitable for this recipe.

2 tablespoons olive oil
1.5kg blade steak, cut into 2cm cubes
1 large brown onion (200g), sliced thickly
2 cloves garlic, crushed
250g button mushrooms, quartered
2 stalks celery (150g), trimmed, sliced thickly
2 x 425g cans crushed tomatoes
½ cup (125ml) dry red wine
1½ cups (375ml) beef stock
2 medium potatoes (400g), quartered
2 large carrots (360g), sliced thickly
2 teaspoons coarsely chopped fresh thyme
200g green beans, trimmed
200g yellow beans, trimmed

1 Heat half the oil in large heavy-based saucepan; cook steak, in batches, over high heat until browned.
2 Heat remaining oil in same pan; cook onion and garlic, stirring, until onion softens. Add mushrooms and celery; cook, stirring, 3 minutes. Return steak to pan with undrained tomatoes, wine and stock; bring to the boil. Reduce heat; simmer, covered, 2 hours.
3 Add potato and carrot; simmer, covered, about 30 minutes or until steak is tender. Stir in thyme.
4 Meanwhile, boil, steam or microwave beans until just tender; drain. Serve beans with stew.

preparation time *10 minutes*
cooking time *2 hours 50 minutes* serves *4*
nutritional count per serving *32.5g total fat (10.8g saturated fat); 3377kJ (808 cal); 27.3g carbohydrate; 90.3g protein; 11.8g fibre*

shanks in five-spice, tamarind and ginger

2 teaspoons five-spice powder
1 teaspoon dried chilli flakes
1 cinnamon stick
2 star anise
¼ cup (60ml) japanese soy sauce
½ cup (125ml) chinese cooking wine
2 tablespoons tamarind concentrate
2 tablespoons brown sugar
8cm piece fresh ginger (40g), grated
2 cloves garlic, chopped coarsely
1¼ cups (310ml) water
8 french-trimmed lamb shanks (2kg)
500g choy sum, chopped into 10cm lengths
150g sugar snap peas, trimmed

1 Preheat oven to 180°C/160°C fan-forced.
2 Dry-fry five-spice, chilli, cinnamon and star anise in small frying pan, stirring, until fragrant. Combine spices with sauce, wine, tamarind, sugar, ginger, garlic and the water in medium jug.
3 Place shanks, in single layer, in large shallow baking dish; drizzle with spice mixture. Roast, uncovered, in oven, turning shanks occasionally, about 2 hours or until meat is almost falling off the bone. Remove shanks from dish; cover to keep warm. Skim excess fat from dish; strain sauce into small saucepan.
4 Meanwhile, boil, steam or microwave choy sum and peas, separately, until tender; drain.
5 Divide vegetables among serving plates; serve with shanks, drizzle with reheated sauce.

preparation time *20 minutes*
cooking time *2 hours 10 minutes* serves *4*
nutritional count per serving *20g total fat (9g saturated fat); 1898kJ (454 cal); 12.1g carbohydrate; 48.3g protein; 3.1g fibre*

osso buco

The name means "hollow bones". Osso Buco is served throughout Italy but is a specialty of Milan.

90g butter
2 medium carrots (240g), chopped finely
2 large brown onions (400g), chopped finely
3 stalks celery (450g), trimmed, chopped finely
2 cloves garlic, crushed
6 pieces osso buco (2kg)
plain flour, for dusting
2 tablespoons olive oil
2 x 410g cans crushed tomatoes
½ cup (125ml) dry red wine
1¾ cups (430ml) beef stock
1 tablespoon finely chopped fresh basil
1 teaspoon finely chopped fresh thyme
1 bay leaf
2.5cm strip lemon rind
¼ cup finely chopped fresh flat-leaf parsley
1 teaspoon grated lemon rind

1 Heat 30g of the butter in large saucepan; cook carrot, onion, celery and half the garlic until onion is golden brown. Remove from heat; transfer vegetables to large ovenproof dish.

2 Coat veal with flour. Heat remaining butter and oil in same pan. Add veal; brown well on all sides. Carefully pack veal on top of vegetables.

3 Meanwhile, preheat oven 180°C/160°C fan-forced.

4 Drain fat from pan. Add undrained tomatoes, wine, stock, basil, thyme, bay leaf and strip of lemon rind; bring sauce to the boil.

5 Pour sauce over veal. Cover casserole; bake in oven about 1½ hours or until veal is tender, stirring occasionally. Serve osso buco sprinkled with combined remaining garlic, parsley and grated lemon rind.

preparation time *30 minutes*
cooking time *2 hours* serves *6*
nutritional count per serving *22.3g total fat (10g saturated fat); 2132kJ (210 cal); 17g carbohydrate; 54.3g protein; 5.6g fibre*

beef stew with parsley dumplings

1kg beef chuck steak, cut into 5cm pieces
2 tablespoons plain flour
2 tablespoons olive oil
20g butter
2 medium brown onions (300g), chopped coarsely
2 cloves garlic, crushed
2 medium carrots (240g), chopped coarsely
1 cup (250ml) dry red wine
2 tablespoons tomato paste
2 cups (500ml) beef stock
4 sprigs fresh thyme
parsley dumplings
1 cup (150g) self-raising flour
50g butter
1 egg, beaten lightly
¼ cup (20g) coarsely grated parmesan cheese
¼ cup finely chopped fresh flat-leaf parsley
⅓ cup (50g) drained sun-dried tomatoes,
    finely chopped
¼ cup (60ml) milk

1 Preheat oven to 180°C/160°C fan-forced.
2 Coat beef in flour; shake off excess. Heat oil in large flameproof dish; cook beef, in batches, until browned.
3 Melt butter in same dish; cook onion, garlic and carrot, stirring, until vegetables soften. Add wine; cook, stirring, until liquid reduces to ¼ cup. Return beef with paste, stock and thyme; bring to the boil. Cover, transfer to oven; cook 1¾ hours.
4 Meanwhile, make parsley dumpling mixture.
5 Remove dish from oven. Drop level tablespoons of dumpling mixture, about 2cm apart, onto top of stew. Cook, uncovered, about 20 minutes or until dumplings are browned lightly and cooked through.
parsley dumplings Place flour in medium bowl; rub in butter. Stir in egg, cheese, parsley, tomato and enough milk to make a soft, sticky dough.
preparation time *30 minutes*
cooking time *2 hours 30 minutes* serves *4*
nutritional count per serving *39.7g total fat (17.4g saturated fat); 3457kJ (827 cal); 43g carbohydrate; 63.9g protein; 6.7g fibre*

borscht with meatballs

Borscht is a fresh beetroot soup, originally from Poland and Russia, made with meat and/or cabbage. Serve it cold or hot, but always with a dollop of sour cream. Ask your butcher to cut the shanks into thirds for you.
Make soup a day ahead to allow the flavours to intensify. Also, make the meatballs the day before; refrigerate, uncooked, covered on a tray. Drop meatballs in reheated soup to cook.

1 tablespoon olive oil
1 small brown onion (80g), chopped coarsely
1 small carrot (70g), chopped coarsely
1 small leek (200g), chopped coarsely
250g cabbage, chopped coarsely
1 large tomato (220g), chopped coarsely
2 medium beetroot (350g), peeled, chopped coarsely
2 veal shanks (1.5kg), trimmed, cut into thirds
1.25 litres (5 cups) water
500g beef mince
½ cup (100g) white medium-grain rice
1 teaspoon sweet paprika
1 small brown onion (80g), chopped finely
3 cloves garlic, crushed
½ cup finely chopped fresh flat-leaf parsley
2 eggs, beaten lightly
½ cup (120g) sour cream
2 tablespoons finely chopped fresh dill

1 Heat oil in large saucepan; cook coarsely chopped onion, carrot, leek, cabbage, tomato and beetroot, stirring, 15 minutes. Add shanks and the water; bring to the boil. Reduce heat; simmer, covered, 1½ hours. Remove shanks; remove and reserve meat from shanks for another use, such as in a soup or stew.
2 Meanwhile, combine mince, rice, paprika, finely chopped onion, garlic, parsley and egg in large bowl; shape rounded teaspoons of mixture into meatballs.
3 Return borscht to the boil; add meatballs. Reduce heat; simmer, uncovered, until meatballs are cooked through.
4 Divide borscht and meatballs among serving bowls; dollop with combined sour cream and dill. Serve with sliced rye or pumpernickel bread.
preparation time *20 minutes*
cooking time *2 hours* serves *4*
nutritional count per serving *31.9g total fat (14.5g saturated fat); 3072kJ (735 cal); 34.2g carbohydrate; 73.4g protein; 8.1g fibre*

braised lamb shanks with white bean purée

Many varieties of already-cooked white beans are available canned, among them cannellini, butter and haricot beans; any of these are suitable for this purée.

1 tablespoon olive oil
8 french-trimmed lamb shanks (2kg)
1 large red onion (300g), chopped coarsely
2 cloves garlic, crushed
1 cup (250ml) chicken stock
2 cups (500ml) water
400g can diced tomatoes
1 tablespoon fresh rosemary leaves
4 anchovy fillets, drained, chopped coarsely
2 large red capsicums (700g)
2 large green capsicums (700g)
white bean purée
20g butter
1 small brown onion (80g), chopped finely
1 clove garlic, crushed
¼ cup (60ml) dry white wine
¾ cup (180ml) chicken stock
2 x 400g cans white beans, rinsed, drained
2 tablespoons cream

1 Heat oil in large deep saucepan; cook lamb, in batches, until browned all over.

2 Cook onion and garlic in same pan, stirring, until onion softens. Add stock, the water, undrained tomatoes, rosemary and anchovy; bring to the boil. Return lamb to pan, reduce heat; simmer, covered, 1 hour, stirring occasionally. Uncover; simmer about 45 minutes or until lamb is tender.

3 Meanwhile, quarter capsicums; discard seeds and membranes. Roast under hot grill, skin-side up, until skin blisters and blackens. Cover capsicum pieces with plastic wrap or paper for 5 minutes; peel away skin then slice capsicum thickly.

4 Meanwhile, make white bean purée.

5 Add capsicum to lamb mixture; cook, uncovered, 5 minutes. Serve lamb on white bean purée.

white bean purée Melt butter in medium frying pan; cook onion and garlic, stirring, until onions softens. Add wine; cook, stirring, until liquid is reduced by half. Add stock and beans; bring to the boil. Reduce heat; simmer, uncovered, about 10 minutes or until liquid is almost evaporated. Blend or process bean mixture and cream until smooth.

preparation time *40 minutes*
cooking time *2 hours 30 minutes* serves *4*
nutritional count per serving *18.8g total fat (8.4g saturated fat); 2312kJ (553 cal); 21g carbohydrate; 72.1g protein; 8.6g fibre*

shepherd's pie

curried sausages

shepherd's pie

30g butter
1 medium brown onion (150g), chopped finely
1 medium carrot (120g), chopped finely
½ teaspoon dried mixed herbs
4 cups (750g) chopped cooked lamb
¼ cup (70g) tomato paste
¼ cup (60ml) tomato sauce
2 tablespoons worcestershire sauce
2 cups (500ml) beef stock
2 tablespoons plain flour
⅓ cup (80ml) water
potato topping
5 medium potatoes (1kg), chopped coarsely
60g butter, chopped
¼ cup (60ml) milk

1 Preheat oven to 200°C/180°C fan-forced. Oil shallow 2.5-litre (10-cup) ovenproof dish.
2 Make potato topping.
3 Heat butter in large saucepan; cook onion and carrot, stirring, until tender. Add mixed herbs and lamb; cook, stirring, 2 minutes. Stir in paste, sauces and stock, then blended flour and water; stir over heat until mixture boils and thickens. Pour mixture into dish.
4 Place heaped tablespoons of potato topping on lamb mixture. Bake, in oven, about 20 minutes or until browned lightly and heated through.
potato topping Boil, steam or microwave potato until tender; drain. Mash with butter and milk until smooth.

preparation time *15 minutes*
cooking time *45 minutes* serves *4*
nutritional count per serving *36.2g total fat (20.2g saturated fat); 2976kJ (712 cal); 44.7g carbohydrate; 48.8g protein; 6.6g fibre*

curried sausages

800g thick beef sausages
20g butter
1 medium brown onion (150g), chopped coarsely
1 tablespoon curry powder
2 teaspoons plain flour
2 large carrots (360g), chopped coarsely
2 stalks celery (300g), trimmed, chopped coarsely
500g baby new potatoes, halved
2 cups (500ml) beef stock
1 cup loosely packed fresh flat-leaf parsley leaves

1 Cook sausages, in batches, in heated large deep frying pan until cooked through. Cut each sausage into thirds.
2 Melt butter in same cleaned pan; cook onion, stirring, until soft. Add curry powder and flour; cook, stirring, 2 minutes.
3 Add vegetables and stock; bring to the boil. Reduce heat; simmer, covered, about 15 minutes or until vegetables are tender. Add sausages; simmer, uncovered, until sauce thickens slightly. Stir in parsley.

preparation time *10 minutes*
cooking time *45 minutes* serves *4*
nutritional count per serving *55.8g total fat (27.3g saturated fat); 3177kJ (760 cal); 29.8g carbohydrate; 30.1g protein; 12.8g fibre*

rogan josh

2 teaspoons ground cardamom

2 teaspoons ground cumin

2 teaspoons ground coriander

1kg boned leg of lamb, trimmed,
    diced into 3cm pieces

20g butter

2 tablespoons vegetable oil

2 medium brown onions (300g), sliced thinly

4cm piece fresh ginger (20g), grated

4 cloves garlic, crushed

2 teaspoons sweet paprika

½ teaspoon cayenne pepper

½ cup (125ml) beef stock

425g can crushed tomatoes

2 bay leaves

2 cinnamon sticks

200g yogurt

¾ cup (110g) toasted slivered almonds

1 fresh long red chilli, sliced thinly

1 Combine cardamom, cumin and coriander in medium bowl, add lamb; toss lamb to coat in spice mixture.

2 Heat butter and half the oil in large deep saucepan; cook lamb, in batches, until browned all over.

3 Heat remaining oil in same pan; cook onion, ginger, garlic, paprika and cayenne over low heat, stirring, until onion softens.

4 Return lamb to pan with stock, undrained tomatoes, bay leaves and cinnamon. Add yogurt, 1 tablespoon at a time, stirring well between each addition; bring to the boil. Reduce heat; simmer, covered, about 1½ hours or until lamb is tender.

5 Remove lamb from heat; sprinkle with nuts and chilli. Serve with a cucumber raita and, if desired, warmed naan bread.

preparation time *20 minutes*

cooking time *2 hours* serves *4*

nutritional count per serving *52.8g total fat (15.9g saturated fat); 3256kJ (779 cal); 11.6g carbohydrate; 62.8g protein; 5.3g fibre*

lamb chop and lentil stew with kumara and carrot mash

1 cup (200g) brown lentils
1 tablespoon vegetable oil
1.5kg lamb neck chops
2 medium brown onions (300g), chopped coarsely
2 cloves garlic, crushed
4 rindless bacon rashers (260g), chopped coarsely
1 teaspoon caraway seeds
2 teaspoons ground cumin
½ cup (125ml) dry red wine
⅓ cup (95g) tomato paste
2 cups (500ml) beef stock
425g can diced tomatoes
½ cup coarsely chopped fresh coriander
kumara and carrot mash
2 medium kumara (800g), chopped coarsely
2 medium carrots (240g), chopped coarsely
1 teaspoon ground cumin
⅓ cup (80ml) buttermilk

1 Cook lentils in large saucepan of boiling water, uncovered, about 15 minutes or until tender; drain.

2 Preheat oven to 180°C/160°C fan-forced.

3 Meanwhile, heat oil in large flameproof casserole dish; cook chops, in batches, until browned. Cook onion, garlic and bacon in same heated pan, stirring, until onion is just browned and bacon is crisp. Add spices; cook, stirring, until fragrant. Add wine, paste, stock and undrained tomatoes; bring to the boil.

4 Return chops to dish; stir in lentils. Cook, covered, in oven, 1 hour 10 minutes.

5 Meanwhile, make kumara and carrot mash.

6 Remove stew from heat; stir in coriander. Serve stew with mash.

kumara and carrot mash Boil, steam or microwave kumara and carrot, separately, until tender; drain. Dry-fry cumin in small frying pan until fragrant. Mash vegetables in large bowl with cumin and buttermilk until smooth.

preparation time *20 minutes*
cooking time *1 hour 45 minutes* serves *4*
nutritional count per serving *47.9g total fat (19.6g saturated fat); 3975kJ (951 cal); 44.1g carbohydrate; 76.1g protein; 9.9g fibre*

glossary

ALLSPICE also known as pimento or jamaican pepper; so-named because it tastes like a combination of nutmeg, cumin, clove and cinnamon – all spices. Is available whole or ground, and used in both sweet and savoury dishes.

BACON RASHERS also known as bacon slices; made from cured smoked pork side.

BASIL an aromatic herb; there are many types, but the most commonly used is sweet, or common, basil.
thai also known as horapa; has small leaves and purplish stems, and a slight licorice or aniseed flavour.

BEANS
black-eyed also known as black-eyed peas or cowpeas; the dried seed of a variant of the snake or yard-long bean. Not too dissimilar to white beans in flavour.
borlotti also known as roman beans or pink beans; can be eaten fresh or dried. Interchangeable with pinto beans because of the similarity in appearance – both are pale pink or beige with dark red streaks.
cannellini small white bean similar in appearance and flavour to great northern, navy or haricot beans, all of which can be substituted for the other.
kidney medium-sized red bean, slightly floury in texture yet sweet in flavour; sold dried or canned.
sprouts also known as bean shoots; tender new growths of assorted beans and seeds germinated for consumption as sprouts. The most readily available are mung bean, soya bean, alfalfa and snow pea sprouts.

BEEF
skirt steak lean, flavourful coarse-grained inner-thigh cut. Needs slow-cooking so is good for stews or casseroles.
shin (gravy beef) cut from the lower shin; commonly used in stews and braises. Also known as a shank.
chuck steak cut from the shoulder and neck; chewy but flavourful and inexpensive. A good cut for braises and stews.

BEETROOT also known as red beets or just beets; firm, round, root vegetable.

BLACK PEPPERCORNS picked when the berry is not quite ripe, then dried until it shrivels and the skin turns dark brown to black. It's the strongest flavoured of all the peppercorn varieties.

BREADCRUMBS
packaged fine-textured, crunchy, purchased white breadcrumbs.
stale one- or two-day-old bread made into crumbs by blending or processing.

BUK CHOY also known as bok choy, pak choi, chinese white cabbage or chinese chard; has a fresh, mild mustard taste. Baby buk choy, also known as pak kat farang or shanghai bok choy, is much smaller and more tender than buk choy.

BUTTER use salted or unsalted (sweet) butter; 125g is equal to one stick (4 ounces).

BUTTERMILK originally the term given to the slightly sour liquid left after butter was churned from cream, today it is made similarly to yogurt. Sold alongside all fresh milk products in supermarkets; despite the implication of its name, it is low in fat.

CAPERS the grey-green buds of a warm climate (usually Mediterranean) shrub, sold either dried and salted or pickled in brine. Baby capers, those picked early, are smaller, fuller-flavoured and more expensive than the full-sized ones. Rinse well before using.

CAPSICUM also known as bell pepper or, simply, pepper. Available in red, green, yellow, orange and purplish-black. Discard seeds and membranes before use.

CAYENNE PEPPER a long, thin-fleshed, extremely hot red chilli usually sold dried and ground.

CELERIAC tuberous root with a brown skin, white flesh and a celery-like flavour. It has a soft, velvety flesh that has the creaminess of potato when mashed, and a subtle celery flavour.

CHEESE
bocconcini walnut-sized, baby mozzarella. Spoils rapidly, so must be kept under refrigeration, in brine, for two days at most.
gruyere a Swiss cheese having small holes and a nutty, slightly salty flavour.
mozzarella a soft, spun-curd cheese. It has a low melting point and wonderfully elastic texture when heated and is used to add texture rather than flavour.
parmesan also known as parmigiano; a hard, grainy, cows-milk cheese. The curd is salted in brine for a month before being aged for up to two years.
pizza a blend of grated mozzarella, cheddar and parmesan cheeses.

ricotta the name for this soft cows-milk cheese roughly translates as 'cooked again'. It's made from whey, a by-product of other cheese-making, to which fresh milk and acid are added.
romano a straw-coloured, cows-milk cheese with a grainy texture. Parmesan can be substituted.

CHICKPEAS also called garbanzos, hummus or channa; an irregularly round, sandy-coloured legume.

CHILLI available in many different types and sizes; generally the smaller the chilli, the hotter it is. Use rubber gloves when seeding and chopping fresh chillies as they can burn your skin. Removing seeds and membranes lessens the heat level.
flakes, dried deep-red, dehydrated chilli slices and whole seeds.
green any unripened chilli; also some varieties that are ripe when green.
long red available both fresh and dried; a generic term used for any moderately hot, long (6cm-8cm), thin chilli.
red thai small, medium hot, and bright red in colour.
powder the Asian variety, made from dried ground thai chillies, is the hottest.

CHINESE COOKING WINE also known as hao hsing or chinese rice wine; made from fermented rice, wheat, sugar and salt with a 13.5 per cent alcohol content. Inexpensive and found in Asian food shops; Use mirin or sherry if you can't find it.

CHOY SUM also known as pakaukeo or flowering cabbage, a member of the buk choy family; easy to identify with its long stems, light green leaves and yellow flowers. Is eaten, stems and all.

CIABATTA in Italian, the word means 'slipper', which is the traditional shape of this popular white bread with a crisp crust.

CORIANDER also known as pak chee, cilantro or chinese parsley; bright-green leafy herb with a pungent flavour. Both the stems and roots of coriander are also used in Thai cooking; wash well before using. Coriander seeds are also available but are no substitute for fresh coriander as the taste is very different.

CORNFLOUR also known as cornstarch; used as a thickening agent in cooking.

COUSCOUS a fine, grain-like cereal product made from semolina.

CREAM
cream we used fresh cream, also known as pure cream and pouring cream, unless otherwise stated. It has no additives unlike commercially thickened cream. Minimum fat content 35%.
sour a thick, commercially cultured, soured cream. Minimum fat content 35%.

CUCUMBER, LEBANESE short, slender and thin-skinned. Probably the most popular variety because of its tender, edible skin, tiny, yielding seeds, and sweet, fresh and flavoursome taste.

CUMIN also known as zeera or comino; has a spicy, nutty flavour. Available in seed form or dried and ground.

CURRY
paste some recipes in this book call for commercially prepared pastes of varying strengths and flavours. Use whichever one suits your heat-tolerance best.
powder a blend of ground spices used for convenience when making Indian food. Can consist of some of the following spices in varying proportions: dried chilli, cinnamon, coriander, cumin, fennel, fenugreek, mace, cardamom and turmeric. Choose mild or hot to suit your taste and the recipe.

EGGPLANT purple-skinned vegetable also known as aubergine.

FIVE-SPICE POWDER a fragrant mixture of ground cinnamon, cloves, star anise, sichuan pepper and fennel seeds. Also known as chinese five-spice.

FLAT-LEAF PARSLEY a flat-leaf variety of parsley also known as continental or italian parsley.

FLOUR
plain all-purpose flour made from wheat.
self-raising plain flour sifted with baking powder in the proportion of 1 cup flour to 2 teaspoons baking powder.

GALANGAL also known as ka, a rhizome with a hot ginger-citrusy flavour; used similarly to ginger and garlic. Available fresh or ground. Sometimes known as thai, laos or siamese ginger. Fresh ginger can be substituted, but the flavour won't be the same.

GARAM MASALA a blend of spices based on cardamom, cinnamon, cloves, coriander, fennel and cumin, roasted and ground together.

GHEE butter that has had its milk solids removed, so can be heated to a high temperature without burning. Also known as clarified butter.

GINGER also known as green or root ginger; the thick root of a tropical plant.

KAFFIR LIME LEAVES also known as bai magrood. Look like two glossy dark green leaves joined end to end, forming a rounded hourglass shape. Used fresh or dried; the dried leaves are less potent so double the number if substituting them for fresh. A strip of fresh lime peel may be substituted for each kaffir lime leaf.

HERBS when specified, we used dried (not ground) herbs in the proportion of 1:4 for fresh herbs (1 teaspoon dried herbs equals 4 teaspoons chopped fresh herbs).

KECAP ASIN see sauces.

KUMARA the Polynesian name of an orange-fleshed sweet potato often confused with yam.

LENTILS (red, brown, yellow) dried pulses often identified by and named after their colour; also known as dhal.

LETTUCE
green oak leaf also known as feuille de chene. Also available as a red leaf.
radicchio burgundy-leafed lettuce with white ribs and a slightly bitter flavour.

MESCLUN a salad mix or gourmet salad mix of assorted young lettuce and other green leaves, including baby spinach leaves, mizuna and curly endive.

MINCE also known as ground meat.

MUSHROOM, BUTTON small, cultivated white mushroom with a delicate flavour.

MUSTARD
dijon also known as french. Pale brown, creamy, distinctively flavoured, fairly mild french mustard.
seeds, black also known as brown mustard seeds; more pungent than the white/yellow variety. Available from health-food stores.
seeds, yellow also known as white mustard seeds; used ground for mustard powder and in most prepared mustards.
wholegrain also known as seeded. A french-style coarse-grain mustard made from crushed mustard seeds and dijon-style mustard.

NOODLES, SOFT RICE a white noodle made from rice flour and vegetable oil; available in varying thicknesses, from thin to broad and flat. Rinse under hot water to remove starch and excess oil before using.

OIL
cooking-oil spray we use a cholesterol-free cooking spray made from canola oil.
olive made from ripened olives. Extra virgin and virgin are the best, while extra light or light refers to taste not fat levels.

ONIONS
brown and white are interchangeable, however, white have a more pungent flesh.
green also known as scallion or, incorrectly, shallot; an immature onion picked before the bulb has formed, having a long, bright-green edible stalk.
red also known as spanish, red spanish or bermuda onion; a sweet-flavoured, large, purple-red onion.
shallots also called french shallots, golden shallots or eschalots; small, brown-skinned, elongated members of the onion family. Grows in tight clusters similar to garlic.
spring onions have small white bulbs and long, narrow green-leafed tops.

PAPRIKA a ground dried sweet red capsicum (bell pepper); there are many types available, including sweet, hot, mild and smoked.

PASTA
angel hair also known as barbina. Long, thin, delicate strands of spaghetti-like pasta. They are called 'capelli d'angelo' in Italian.
fettuccine long ribbon pasta.
lasagne sheets, fresh thinly rolled wide sheets of plain or flavoured pasta; they do not requiring par-boiling prior to being used in cooking.
macaroni tube-shaped pasta available in various sizes.
orecchiette small disc-shaped pasta, translates literally as 'little ears'.
penne the Italian name of this pasta means pen, a reference to its nib-like, pointy ends. Penne comes in smooth (lisce) or ridged (rigate), and a variety of sizes.
rigatoni a form of tube-shaped pasta larger than penne. Usually ridged, but the tube's end does not terminate at an angle, like penne's does.
risoni small rice-shape pasta; very similar to another small pasta, orzo.

PEARL BARLEY a nutritious grain that has had its outer husk (bran) removed, and been steamed and polished before being used in cooking.

PINE NUTS also known as pignoli; not in fact a nut but a small, cream-coloured kernel from pine cones.

PIZZA BASES pre-packaged for home-made pizzas. They come in a variety of sizes (snack or family) and thicknesses (thin and crispy or thick), and taste great with your favourite pizza toppings.

POLENTA also known as cornmeal; a flour-like cereal made of dried corn (maize) sold ground in different textures. Also the name of the dish made from it.

POTATOES
baby new also known as chats; not a separate variety but an early harvest with very thin skin.
king edward slightly plump with a rosy skin; great mashed.
russet burbank also known as idaho; russet in colour and used for baking.
sebago oval shaped, white skinned potato; good fried, mashed and baked.

RICE
arborio small, round-grain rice, well-suited to absorb a large amount of liquid; especially suitable for risottos.
long-grain an elongated grain that remains separate when cooked; most popular steaming rice in Asia.
medium-grain previously sold as calrose rice; extremely versatile rice that can be substituted for short- or long-grain rices.

SAUCES
barbecue a spicy, tomato-based sauce used to marinate or as a condiment.
fish also called nam pla or nuoc nam; made from pulverised salted fermented fish, most often anchovies. Has a pungent smell and strong taste, so use sparingly.
piri-piri a hot West African sauce made from dried and soaked piri-piri chillies; used as a condiment to accompany many West African soups and stews. The origin of this sauce is thought to be Portuguese, but it's now well-established as a classic West African condiment. It's available in bottles from delis and supermarkets.
soy made from fermented soya beans. Several variations are available in most supermarkets and Asian food stores.
japanese an all-purpose low-sodium soy sauce made with more wheat content than its Chinese counterparts; fermented in barrels and aged. Possibly the best table soy, and the one to choose if you only want one variety.
kecap asin a thick and salty dark soy sauce with a strong flavour; used in Malaysian and Indonesian cooking.
light a fairly thin, pale but salty tasting sauce; used in dishes in which the natural colour of the ingredients is to be maintained. Not to be confused with salt-reduced or low-sodium soy sauces.

tamari a thick, dark soy sauce made mainly from soya beans without the wheat used in standard soy sauce.
tomato pasta a prepared sauce made from a blend of tomatoes, herbs and spices.
worcestershire a dark coloured sauce made from garlic, soy sauce, tamarind, onions, molasses, lime, anchovies, vinegar and seasonings.

SAUSAGES minced (ground) meat seasoned with salt and spices, mixed with cereal and packed into casings. Also known as snags or bangers.

SILVER BEET also known as blettes and swiss chard and, incorrectly, spinach.

SNOW PEA SPROUTS tender new growths of snow peas; also known as mange tout.

SPINACH also known as english spinach and, incorrectly, silver beet.

SPLIT PEAS also known as field peas; green or yellow pulse grown especially for drying, split in half along a centre seam. Used in soups, stews and, occasionally, spiced and cooked on their own.

STAR ANISE dried star-shaped pod having an astringent aniseed flavour; used to favour stocks and marinades. Available whole and ground, it is an essential ingredient in five-spice powder.

STOCK available in cans, bottles or tetra packs. Stock cubes or powder can be used. As a guide, 1 teaspoon of stock powder or 1 small crumbled stock cube mixed with 1 cup (250ml) water will give a fairly strong stock. Be aware of the salt and fat content of stock cubes and powders and prepared stocks.

SUGAR
brown an extremely soft, finely granulated sugar retaining molasses for its characteristic colour and flavour.
caster also known as superfine or finely granulated table sugar.
palm also known as nam tan pip, jaggery, jawa or gula melaka; made from the sap of the sugar palm tree. Light brown to black in colour and usually sold in rock-hard cakes; the sugar of choice in Indian and most South-East Asian cooking. Substitute with brown sugar if unavailable.
white a coarse, granulated table sugar, also known as crystal sugar.

SUGAR SNAP PEAS also known as honey snap peas; fresh small pea that can be eaten whole, pod and all.

SULTANAS dried grapes, also known as golden raisins.

TAMARI see sauces.

TAMARIND CONCENTRATE commercial distillation of tamarind pulp into a thick condensed paste. Has a sweet/sour, slightly astringent taste. Use straight from the container, with no soaking or straining; can be diluted with water according to taste. Found in Asian supermarkets.

TOFU also known as bean curd, an off-white, custard-like product made from the 'milk' of crushed soya beans; comes fresh as soft or firm. Leftover fresh tofu can be refrigerated in water (which is changed daily) for up to four days.
silken refers to the method by which tofu is made – strained through silk.

TOMATO
paste triple-concentrated tomato purée used to flavour soups, stews, sauces and casseroles.
semi-dried partially-dried tomato pieces in olive oil; softer and juicier than sun-dried, these are not a preserve, so do not keep as long as sun-dried.
sun-dried we used sun-dried tomatoes packaged in oil, unless specified otherwise.

TORTILLAS thin, round unleavened bread originating in Mexico. Two kinds are available, one made from wheat flour and the other from corn.

TURMERIC also known as kamin, a rhizome related to galangal and ginger, must be grated or pounded to release its somewhat acrid aroma and pungent flavour. Known for the golden colour it imparts to the dishes of which it's a part. Fresh turmeric can be substituted with the more common dried powder (use 2 teaspoons of ground turmeric plus a teaspoon of sugar for every 20g of fresh turmeric called for in a recipe.) It is intensely pungent in taste but is not hot.

VINEGAR
balsamic originally from Modena, Italy, there are now many balsamic vinegars on the market ranging in pungency and quality. Quality can be determined up to a point by price; use the most expensive sparingly. It is a deep rich brown colour with a sweet/sour flavour.
brown malt made from fermented malt and beech shavings.
cider (apple cider) made from fermented apples.
white made from spirit of cane sugar.
white wine made from white wine.

WHITE FISH FILLET blue-eye, bream, flathead, swordfish, ling, whiting, jewfish, snapper or sea perch are all good choices. Check for any small pieces of bone in the fillets and use tweezers to remove them.

WOMBOK also known as petsai or peking or chinese cabbage. Elongated in shape with pale green, crinkly leaves, this is the most common cabbage in South-East Asian cooking.

YEAST a 7g (¼oz) sachet of dried yeast (2 teaspoons) is equal to 15g (½oz) compressed yeast if substituting one for the other.

ZUCCHINI also known as courgette; small, pale- or dark-green, yellow or white vegetable belonging to the squash family. Harvested when young, its edible flowers can be stuffed then deep-fried or oven-baked to make a delicious appetiser.

conversion chart

MEASURES

One Australian metric measuring cup holds approximately 250ml; one Australian metric tablespoon holds 20ml; one Australian metric teaspoon holds 5ml.

The difference between one country's measuring cups and another's is within a two- or three-teaspoon variance, and will not affect your cooking results. North America, New Zealand and the United Kingdom use a 15ml tablespoon.

All cup and spoon measurements are level. The most accurate way of measuring dry ingredients is to weigh them. When measuring liquids, use a clear glass or plastic jug with the metric markings.

We use large eggs with an average weight of 60g.

DRY MEASURES

METRIC	IMPERIAL
15g	½oz
30g	1oz
60g	2oz
90g	3oz
125g	4oz (¼lb)
155g	5oz
185g	6oz
220g	7oz
250g	8oz (½lb)
280g	9oz
315g	10oz
345g	11oz
375g	12oz (¾lb)
410g	13oz
440g	14oz
470g	15oz
500g	16oz (1lb)
750g	24oz (1½lb)
1kg	32oz (2lb)

LIQUID MEASURES

METRIC	IMPERIAL
30ml	1 fluid oz
60ml	2 fluid oz
100ml	3 fluid oz
125ml	4 fluid oz
150ml	5 fluid oz (¼ pint/1 gill)
190ml	6 fluid oz
250ml	8 fluid oz
300ml	10 fluid oz (½ pint)
500ml	16 fluid oz
600ml	20 fluid oz (1 pint)
1000ml (1 litre)	1¾ pints

LENGTH MEASURES

METRIC	IMPERIAL
3mm	⅛in
6mm	¼in
1cm	½in
2cm	¾in
2.5cm	1in
5cm	2in
6cm	2½in
8cm	3in
10cm	4in
13cm	5in
15cm	6in
18cm	7in
20cm	8in
23cm	9in
25cm	10in
28cm	11in
30cm	12in (1ft)

OVEN TEMPERATURES

These oven temperatures are only a guide for conventional ovens. For fan-forced ovens, check the manufacturer's manual.

	°C (CELSIUS)	°F (FAHRENHEIT)	GAS MARK
Very slow	120	250	½
Slow	150	275-300	1-2
Moderately slow	160	325	3
Moderate	180	350-375	4-5
Moderately hot	200	400	6
Hot	220	425-450	7-8
Very hot	240	475	9

index

If you like this cookbook, you'll love these...

These are just a small selection of titles available in
The Australian Women's Weekly range on sale at selected
newsagents, supermarkets or online at www.acpbooks.com.au

also available in bookstores...

ACP BOOKS

General manager Christine Whiston
Editorial director Susan Tomnay
Creative director & designer Hieu Chi Nguyen
Senior editor Wendy Bryant
Food director Pamela Clark
Test Kitchen manager Belinda Farlow
Director of sales Brian Cearnes
Marketing manager Bridget Cody
Communications and brand manager Xanthe Roberts
Senior business analyst Rebecca Varela
Circulation manager Jama Mclean
Operations manager David Scotto
Production manager Victoria Jefferys
European rights enquiries Laura Bamford lbamford@acpuk.com

ACP Books are published by ACP Magazines a division
of PBL Media Pty Limited
Group editorial director, Women's lifestyle Pat Ingram
Group publishing & sales director, Women's lifestyle Lynette Phillips
Commercial manager, Women's lifestyle Seymour Cohen
Marketing director, Women's lifestyle Matthew Dominello
Research director, Women's lifestyle Justin Stone
PBL Media, Chief Executive Officer Ian Law

Published by ACP Books, a division of ACP Magazines Ltd,
54 Park St, Sydney; GPO Box 4088, Sydney, NSW 2001.
phone (02) 9282 8618; fax (02) 9267 9438.
acpbooks@acpmagazines.com.au; www. acpbooks.com.au
Printed by Dai Nippon in Korea.

Australia Distributed by Network Services,
phone +61 2 9282 8777; fax +61 2 9264 3278;
networkweb@networkservicescompany.com.au
United Kingdom Distributed by Australian Consolidated Press (UK),
phone (01604) 642 200; fax (01604) 642 300; books@acpuk.com
New Zealand Distributed by Netlink Distribution Company,
phone (9) 366 9966; ask@ndc.co.nz
South Africa Distributed by PSD Promotions,
phone (27 11) 392 6065/6/7; fax (27 11) 392 6079/80;
orders@psdprom.co.za
Canada Distributed by Publishers Group Canada
phone (800) 663 5714; fax (800) 565 3770; service@raincoast.com

Title: Smart food / compiler: Pamela Clark.
ISBN: 978 1 86396 924 6 (pbk.)
Notes: Includes index.
Subjects: Low budget cookery. Cookery.
Other Authors/Contributors: Clark, Pamela.
Dewey Number: 641.552
© ACP Magazines Ltd 2009
ABN 18 053 273 546

The publishers would like to thank the following for props used
in photography: Chee Soon & Fitzgerald, No Chintz.

To order books, phone 136 116 (within Australia)
or order online at www.acpbooks.com.au
Send recipe enquiries to:
recipeenquiries@acpmagazines.com.au